Arup Associates

TWENTIETH CENTURY ARCHITECTS

Arup Associates

Kenneth Powell

Historic England

C20

RIBA ⊞ Publishing

The Twentieth Century Society

Published by Historic England,
The Engine House, Fire Fly Avenue,
Swindon SN2 2EH
www.HistoricEngland.org.uk
Historic England is a Government service championing England's heritage
and giving expert, constructive advice.

The views expressed in this book are those of the author and not necessarily
those of Historic England and/or the Twentieth Century Society.

First published 2018
ISBN 978-1-84802-367-3 paperback

British Library Cataloguing in Publication data
A CIP catalogue record for this book is available from the British Library.

The right of Kenneth Powell to be identified as author of this work has
been asserted by him in accordance with the Copyright, Designs and
Patents Act 1988.

Series editors: Timothy Brittain-Catlin, Barnabas Calder, Elain Harwood
and Alan Powers

Brought to publication by Sarah Enticknap, Publishing, Historic England

Typeset in Quadraat, 10.75pt
Edited by Anne McDowall
Indexed by Sue Vaughan
Page layout by Rod Harrison, Ledgard Jepson Ltd

Printed in the UK by Gomer Press

Front Cover: No. 1 Finsbury Avenue, City of London, 1981–4

Frontispiece: George Thomson Building, Corpus Christi College, Cambridge

Back Cover: Lunch at the model shop, *c* 1980

Contents

Foreword

When I was a student in the mid-1970s, I had Arup Associates on something of a pedestal. The form of the architecture resonated with ideas that had already caught my attention, especially the spatial synchronisation with structure and its empathy with the environment, but it also seemed to emulate the more humane direction that had emerged once the commanding influence of the modern masters had been challenged. The more I found out about this practice, the more interesting it became. Although Philip Dowson's name was known outside the firm, it was clearly not a conventional architectural practice led by one or two founding partners; indeed, it had been spawned by a leading engineering firm – Ove Arup & Partners, no less – and had pioneered multidisciplinary working. For an idealistic architecture student, the idea of the engineers and architects working in a combined team was unarguable, and it seemed to underpin the distinctive tectonic language of the architecture to which I was so attracted.

During a speculative job-seeking trip to London after graduation in 1977, I called in at Arup Associates to see if I could get an interview, and so began a ten-year 'apprenticeship', the impact of which is still very much with me today.

Arup Associates was everything I had imagined and more. Working on a stream of large-scale buildings with Peter Foggo's group, I found myself at the centre of an industry, not just a profession, where innovation and high levels of achievement were applied at all stages of the design and construction process. I could see immediately the chemistry between the architects and engineers, but I had not appreciated the integral role of the administrator and quantity surveyors, who occupied the centre of each group's studio, with the design disciplines around the perimeter. Nor had I expected the role of contractors to be so prominent, with semi-permanent links to a handful of like-minded firms (such as Bovis and Josef Gartner) extending the pan-industry ideals to specialist manufacturers and new types of contracts.

These buildings were winning countless awards for their architectural excellence, so the connection between the ends and the means seemed resolute. One project after another was executed with such speed and efficiency that I began to think this was normal, and it was only later, once I had formed Bennetts Associates with my wife Denise in 1987, that the reality of our fragmented, argumentative construction industry became apparent.

Gateway House 1, Basingstoke, completed in 1976

For more than 20 years, exasperated governments have called for radical industry reform, but Arup Associates was a powerful exemplar all along.

Although Arup Associates' location in Soho Square symbolised for a time its independence from Ove Arup & Partners in Fitzroy Street, the spirit of the firm had descended directly from the great man himself. It had a liberal attitude and aspired to a relatively flat hierarchy, with all members of the team empowered to contribute on merit. The highest standards of ethical and professional behaviour were beyond debate, and there were many examples during my time when the firm did 'the right thing' rather than be led by commercial considerations. The humanity of Arup's approach became the basis for more than 50 years of exceptional output.

But in one respect, Arup Associates has been an enigma. I have long questioned my initial assumption that the method led automatically to architecture of distinction, for, despite its reputation for egalitarianism, the force of key personalities underpinned the finest buildings. There were many talented individuals who drove the design process, but their contribution was downplayed in the interests of the collective effort. During my decade with the practice, for example, the creative tension between Philip Dowson and Peter Foggo was legendary, but it raised the level of architectural discourse and exposed through their architecture how the romantics and the pragmatists could co-exist within a common intellectual framework. Engineers such as Derek Sugden and Bob Hobbs were equally influential, quietly helping to realise ambitions and nurture younger talents.

In a world that increasingly revolves around individuals, Arup Associates has bravely held on to an identity built exclusively on its output, but the absence of articles or recorded speeches by its leading characters has sometimes made it difficult for history to record the practice's work with perspective. How appropriate it is, then, that Ken Powell's text sheds direct light on the many architects whose work is now included in a volume in the Twentieth Century Architects series.

RAB BENNETTS

Acknowledgements

This book was made possible by a generous donation from Arup Associates, although the practice had no formal involvement in the book's contents and the views expressed within. I am grateful to many former members of Arup Associates for sharing with me their memories and thoughts on the work of the practice. It was a particular privilege to meet with Sir Philip Dowson and Derek Sugden, two of its founding partners, who sadly did not live to see this book published. Derek was a particular inspiration, and the book is dedicated to his memory.

Among others who generously gave of their time, I should like to thank Rab Bennetts, Mike Bonner, John Braithwaite, Mick Brundle, James Burland, Don Ferguson, Richard Frewer, Alistair Gourlay, Nicholas Hare, Dave King, Michael Lowe, Clarence McDonald, Tony Marriott, Stuart Mercer, Sam Price, Terry Raggett, Graeme Smart, Tim Sturgis, Rodney Tan, Tony Taylor, David Thomas, Peter Warburton and Crispin Wride.

Sir Stuart Lipton and Sir Jack Zunz provided valuable insights into the history of the practice.

Professor Ian Jones and Tony Burbery gave me a comprehensive tour of the Metallurgy and Minerals Building at the University of Birmingham. Professor Peter Carolin of Corpus Christi College, Cambridge, introduced me to the Leckhampton Building and facilitated access to college archives. Anne Manuel and Kate O'Donnell at Somerville College, Oxford, and Michael Riordan at St John's College, Oxford, steered me through their own archives. Joe Williams of Computershare Ltd showed me around the former CEGB offices in Bristol, which his company has successfully adapted for their use. Mick Brundle organised illuminating visits to Plantation Place and Ropemaker.

Dr Alistair Fair was a valuable source of information on Somerville College and provided a photograph of Philip Dowson's first built work, the bus shelter in Geldeston. I am grateful to Simon Bradley and Charles O'Brien of Pevsner Architectural Guides for generously sharing information.

I am grateful to Michael Beaven and Declan O'Carroll of Arup Associates for my introduction to the practice and for a fruitful collaboration on the production of the book published to mark its 50th anniversary in 2013.

I am particularly grateful to Joanne Ronaldson of Arup Associates for providing so many of the illustrations for the book and for much helpful advice. Photographs from Derek Sugden's archive were kindly provided by his widow, Katherine Douglas, and his daughter and son-in-law, Caroline and Roger Hillier. A meeting with Sir Philip Dowson's daughters, Katharine Dowson and Anna

York Shipley factory at Basildon, 1959–62

Nasmyth, added much to my knowledge of Philip's life. Lilian Foggo kindly sourced a photograph of her late husband, Peter Foggo.

Anne McDowall edited the text with precision and sensitivity, and Sarah Enticknap of Historic England oversaw the process of bringing the book to publication. The excellent new photography by Steve Baker, Anna Bridson, James O Davies, Pat Payne and Chris Redgrave of Historic England has added a new dimension to appreciation of Arup Associates' work. Thanks are also due to the staff of the Robert Elwall Photographs Collection at the Royal Institute of British Architects.

Finally, special thanks is due to Dr Elain Harwood of Historic England, as editor of the 20th Century Architects series, for encouragement, invaluable advice and for a meticulous edit of my text.

Lloyd's of London HQ at Chatham, 1973–76

Introduction

Throughout his long career, (Sir) Ove Nyquist Arup (1895–1988) was preoccupied by the relationship between architecture and engineering, addressing the issue in writings and lectures. As a young man, he had considered training as an architect, but decided that he lacked the requisite design skills and 'artistic ability', so opted instead for engineering. Addressing the RIBA in 1966, on his receipt of the Royal Gold Medal, he spoke with characteristic modesty of his 'long apprenticeship as an architectural student' – the three decades of collaboration with architects that had begun with his work with Berthold Lubetkin in the 1930s.[1]

Arup's pursuit of integrated or 'total' design grew out of his vision of teamwork, where all the members of the team 'want to help to produce good architecture, architecture in depth so to speak – not just artificially imposed formalism or applied make-up – as well as efficient function and economy … all the members have to forget part of their training and acquire new understanding and skills. Barriers – which are astoundingly solid and high – must be broken down'.[2]

Above: Ove Arup in typically relaxed mode

Opposite: The development at Warwick Road, Kensington, completed in 1976, combined a council works depot with social housing

The old divide between architecture and engineering – or 'art' and 'function', as Arup defined it – still rigorously maintained in the 19th century, seemed ludicrous to the Modern Movement, to which the work of Brunel and Paxton was as much architecture as that of Pugin or Scott. But even in the post-war years, the professional institutions in Britain seemed desperate to maintain the traditional barriers. It was this ingrained thinking that Arup challenged, becoming, in Andrew Saint's words, 'the greatest of the peacemakers' in the old war between architects and engineers, someone who stood for 'a fresh pattern of partnership between architect and engineer'.³ Arup's ideal was to achieve the perfect union of design and construction, and this drove his collaboration with architects on projects such as the Brynmawr Rubber Factory, the Spa Green and Hallfield housing estates and the Smithsons' school at Hunstanton.

The Brynmawr Rubber Factory in South Wales, a dramatic example of Arup engineering, 1946–51

The circumstances of the years immediately following the Second World War were conducive to the erosion of professional divisions. The urgent need to replace destroyed housing and industrial buildings, and to build schools and hospitals embodying the ideals of the Welfare State, made old rivalries seem less relevant. Arup's practice, founded in 1946, was well equipped to design practical buildings that could be constructed quickly and to tight budgets. Its contribution under Ronald Jenkins and Ronald 'Bob' Hobbs was critical to the success of major industrial projects designed in collaboration with architectural practices, such as the Brynmawr Rubber Factory in South Wales (with Architects' Co-Partnership) and the Bank of England printing plant at Loughton, Essex (with Easton & Robertson). Bob Hobbs, who joined Ove Arup & Partners in 1948, subsequently led the Building Group within the practice, the main focus of which was factories for new-style industries, generally in city-edge or new-town locations.

Ove Arup's determination to produce buildings that were works of architecture led to the recruitment, in 1953, of Philip Dowson and Francis Pym, fresh from the Architectural Association. In the same year, Hobbs also recruited Derek Sugden, a highly experienced young engineer with particular expertise in steelwork, and thus was formed the triumvirate to which Ove Arup entrusted the leadership of the architectural practice launched formally in 1963. These three, with Arup himself, were to be the first partners.

The factory projects of the 1950s and early 1960s were fruitful collaborations by a Building Group of around 12 architects, engineers and quantity surveyors. Dowson's architectural flair came to the fore in a project such as the laboratories at Duxford for CIBA (Chemische Industrie Basel). For Derek Sugden, a lifelong socialist, the industrial architecture of the post-war era was about creating humane working spaces – light and airy and a far remove from the 'satanic mills' of the Victorian age. The industrial theme in Arup Associates' work remained significant in subsequent decades, culminating in the Horizon Factory at Nottingham, completed in 1971 and designed by a team led by Peter Foggo, the fifth partner in the practice from 1966. The project was innovative in many respects, not least in pioneering a new approach to building procurement, which became a key feature of Foggo's office projects of the 1980s. The new industrial sector emerging in Britain from the 1960s onwards saw research, development and manufacture combined on one site in what were, in effect, new building types. The computer industry led the way, and Arup Associates was well equipped to respond to the needs of the big American technology company IBM when it came to Britain, developing new facilities around the Solent that resembled university campuses rather than traditional industrial complexes. IBM became a core client for the practice over a period of more than 15 years.

The Metallurgy and Minerals Building at the University of Birmingham marked a breakthrough in the design of laboratories that incorporated service ducts within the striking architectural framework of a tartan grid

It is tempting, perhaps, to see the work of Arup Associates as a series of phases in which particular building types and clients came to the fore. In contrast with other leading post-war practices, Arup Associates emerged in the 1960s without having to go through the experience of first building schools or public housing. The exceptions are the Point Royal tower in Bracknell and the housing ingeniously incorporated into the Kensington Central Depot, Warwick Road, completed in 1976.

However, one area where the practice made its mark was that of university accommodation. Philip Dowson's appointment to design new residential buildings for Somerville College, Oxford, led to the establishment of the new partnership as a multidisciplinary architectural practice. A major commission from Corpus Christi College, Cambridge, followed and in 1967 Dowson was appointed to design a very large development for Oxford's richest college, St John's. Though subsequently reduced in scale, the project remained the most ambitious of the Oxbridge college schemes. Dowson clearly enjoyed the ethos of Oxbridge, and all these projects produced well-crafted buildings that deferred to context while sharing a common structural grid. Tim Sturgis, who worked with Philip Dowson on all the college projects, recalled that 'the inspiration was partly Nervi and Maillart, partly Arts and Crafts, and partly the directness of traditional vernacular buildings … We were trying to develop a new vocabulary of construction suited to the then current technical possibilities and their limitations. It should have the richness and humanity of those old buildings which we all admired'.[4]

There were also teaching buildings for the universities of Oxford and Cambridge. But arguably the most memorable of Arup Associates' university projects is one that is anything but contextual. The Metallurgy and Materials Building at Birmingham University, completed in 1966 and designed by a team that included Dowson, Hobbs and Max Fordham, saw a pioneering use of the 'tartan grid', integrating structure and services and a strategy revisited many times in subsequent projects. As a second-generation post-war practice, Arup Associates was less obviously influenced by the iconic pre-war works of the European Modern Movement than by the work of Mies van der Rohe, Skidmore, Owings & Merrill and Louis Kahn in the United States. Kahn, in particular, was a potent influence, and his own interest in the integration of structure and services to create a distinctive architectural language has a parallel in the work of Arup Associates from the Birmingham project onwards.

With the higher education expansion programme of the 1960s in full flow, Arup Associates was commissioned for another major building on the Birmingham campus and for buildings at Leicester (the 17-storey Attenborough Building), Surrey and Loughborough universities, the latter the subject of a giant master plan based on the tartan grid. Dowson was to return to Cambridge, and to his alma mater, Clare College, in the 1980s to design the Forbes Mellon Library, a project that seemed to some of his colleagues to defer too much to the then current post-modernist fashion.

The Attenborough Tower at the University of Leicester, 1964–70

In common with its peers – practices such as those of Powell & Moya, Denys Lasdun, and Howell, Killick, Partridge & Amis – Arup Associates shunned the world of property development. The speculative office boom of the 1960s instead provided plentiful work for 'commercial' practices, not least that of Richard Seifert. Philip Dowson characterised the typical modern office block as 'the unacceptable face of architecture, lending its name to commercial exploitation. The visible and outward expression of the inner logic of what one client called "the maximisation of space utilisation ... indifferent to the real purpose which should be to provide a good place for people to work in"'. As an alternative to the anonymity of the typical modern office, Dowson offered a vision of 'working communities', diverse in their needs – 'the buildings that clothe them should reflect the character of these differences. The designs should ensure that they are not ironed out and obliterated by considerations of adaptability, flexibility, maximum net usable area, or whatever else, if they are to have a human reference'.[5]

Bespoke office schemes, designed for occupation by prestige clients, offered the opportunity to create buildings that recognised the need for individual as well as corporate identity. Big British companies, including Lloyd's of London, the Central Electricity Generating Board, Lloyds Bank, Wiggins Teape, Legal & General and Royal Life, commissioned costly headquarters buildings from the practice. Stylistically diverse, in tune with a new pluralist spirit – and, with the Legal & General project, a bold essay in full-blooded post-modern classicism – these projects provided scope for innovative services design, and the Lloyd's of London building at Chatham and CEGB's regional headquarters in Bristol were models of sustainability. A similar agenda drove Gateway 2 at Basingstoke, the second building there for Wiggins Teape, designed by Peter Foggo's Group 2.

Although Arup Associates had made a foray into the field of speculative offices a decade earlier, with a scheme in Cannon Street for Trafalgar House, Foggo's work for developer Stuart Lipton at Finsbury Avenue and Broadgate seemed to take the practice into a new area. Foggo was undeterred by the challenge of speculative office design and boldly seized the opportunities offered by the building boom of the 1980s. Rejecting 'pseudo-ethical notions', he embraced American-style fast-track construction – while insisting that 'we must distinguish between fast building and fast designing'.[6] By involving his team in the design of the prefabricated components that were fundamental to the success of his work at Finsbury Avenue and Broadgate, Foggo was able to maintain control over the quality of the completed building, though interior spaces were left to be fitted out to the requirements of incoming tenants. It was an agenda at odds, it might seem, with Philip Dowson's ideals, but one that gave a new dynamism to Arup Associates.

Although Foggo left Arup Associates in 1989 to establish his own practice, more big speculative office schemes were to come, notably the Plantation Place and Ropemaker developments for British Land. But Arup Associates' hopes to create a new quarter at the very heart of the City of London were dashed when its scheme for Paternoster Square was abandoned in the face of criticism from the Prince of Wales.

Industrial buildings, university projects and offices have formed the mainstay of Arup Associates' workload over more than half a century. But there have also been significant cultural projects – the expansion of the Imperial War Museum, for example. Derek Sugden's remodelling of Snape Maltings for the Aldeburgh Festival is one of the most memorable of all Arup Associates' buildings, a classic example of creative reuse. Under Sugden, the practice restored historic theatres in Glasgow and Buxton and renovated a splendid Georgian church as a rehearsal facility for several leading orchestras.

Arup Associates' work in the last decade lies beyond the scope of this book, with many major projects far from Britain. Big sporting projects in the Middle and Far East have built on the success of those nearer home, notably the Manchester Etihad stadium. Having celebrated its 50th birthday in 2013 – and with a history extending back a further decade – Arup Associates is something of a survivor among leading British architectural practices. The practices with which it competed in its early years have ceased to exist. It has weathered the 1970s crisis of modernism – which was the guiding light to Ove Arup in the 1930s – and the rise of post-modernism in the 1980s. 'High-tech' practices – those of Foster, Rogers, Grimshaw and Hopkins – became its competitors in turn, yet in its pioneering integration of structure and services, Arup Associates led the way where others followed. In its commitment to rational design responding to practical needs, it resisted the pursuit of pure form – of 'art' ignoring 'function', as Ove Arup might have seen it – characteristic of some fashionable architects of the early 21st century. Arup Associates' huge and diverse body of work commands respect and emulation at a time when the ideals on which the practice was founded badly need to be restated.

1 Origins and industrial buildings

The story of Arup Associates begins with Ove Arup and his vision of 'a fresh
pattern of partnership between architect and engineer'.[1] Arup was born in 1895
in Newcastle-upon-Tyne, the son of a Danish father serving as a veterinary consul
and a Norwegian mother, and spent his early years in Hamburg. He studied
philosophy and mathematics briefly at Copenhagen University before moving
on to the city's Polytechnic Institute (now the Technical University of Denmark).
He was attracted by the idea of becoming an architect, but decided that he lacked
the appropriate skills and concluded that 'it wouldn't be the worse thing to
happen, to become an engineer'.[2] In 1922, duly qualified after six years of study,
he joined the Danish contractors Christiani & Nielsen, whose expertise in the
use of reinforced concrete had won the company an international reputation.
Arup was sent to work first in its Hamburg office and then to London, where he
worked initially on docks and industrial buildings and where, in 1925, he married
Ruth Sørenson, daughter of the managing director of the Danish water authority,
himself an eminent engineer.

The year 1932 saw Arup's career move in a new direction as he progressed
from routine engineering problems towards the use of concrete in modern
architectural construction, something in which Britain lagged behind other
European countries. Acting as both engineer and architect, he designed a café
on the beach at Canvey Island on the Thames Estuary, a building he later dismissed as 'architecture on the cheap by an amateur architect', but which stands
as a significant pioneering work of the Modern Movement in Britain. Also in
1932, Arup met Berthold Lubetkin, who had moved to Britain from Paris in the
previous year, launching the architectural practice Tecton. The introduction to
Lubetkin – who wanted help with his first building for London Zoo, the Gorilla
House – came via the Danish contractor Olaf Kier, and in 1934, Arup joined
Kier's company as Design Director.

The collaboration with Lubetkin realised, at least for a time, Ove Arup's ideal
of a partnership between art and technology, fused to produce what Arup later
described as 'total design'. Arup moved in architectural circles, joining both
the Architectural Association and the newly established Modern Architectural
Research (MARS) Group. He worked with Tecton on the Penguin Pool at the
Zoo, the Finsbury Health Centre and the Highpoint apartment blocks. Tecton,
he later recalled, 'was a group of people with a sense of mission, a common

Detail of the Horizon Factory, Nottingham, 1968–71

The café at Canvey Island, Essex, designed by Ove Arup and built in 1932–3

cause to create a new architecture which would cast off the tyranny of "Beaux Arts" and all the old styles for all time and replace it with a new international style based on our new technology, which was capable of satisfying the needs and aspirations of mankind if used with reason and justice'.[3] Until their relationship cooled at the end of the war, Arup and Lubetkin shared an idealistic vision of architecture as a progressive force in society. Derek Sugden, who joined the Arup practice in 1953, wrote of Ove Arup as 'philosophical and practical, conformist and anarchist, complex and uncomplicated, serious and playful, wise and impetuous, a spiritual materialist'.[4]

Ove Arup & Partners

In 1938, Arup left Kier to form a partnership with a cousin, Arne Arup. The partnership was dissolved in 1946 (though it took until 1952 to sort out the details), when Ove Arup founded Ove N Arup, Consulting Engineers; in 1949, the practice became Ove Arup & Partners, the other founding partners being Ronald Jenkins, Geoffrey Wood and Andrew Young. It quickly established itself as a major force in the post-war rebuilding of Britain, collaborating with the Architects' Co-Partnership, Denys Lasdun, Peter and Alison Smithson, Maxwell

Fry and Jane Drew, and Basil Spence, among others. Their schools, hospitals and housing projects formed part of an idealistic agenda of reconstruction that was in tune with Arup's own socialist convictions. In some projects, the engineering input to the designs was fundamental to the realisation of the architect's vision. A notable example was the Brynmawr Rubber Factory in South Wales, completed in 1951 to designs by the Architects' Co-Partnership. The defining feature of the building (sadly demolished in 2001) was the series of nine concrete shell roofs covering the production area, conceived by an Arup team led by Ronald Jenkins.

Just as Ove Arup had acted as both architect and engineer for the Canvey Island café, so Ove Arup & Partners assumed both roles for a number of projects. Perhaps significantly, these were industrial buildings, constructed to tight schedules and often very limited budgets, that could have been seen as purely functional and therefore detached from the aesthetic concerns of architects. This first generation of buildings designed by what was to become Arup Associates combined a concern for structural economy, flexibility and the efficient integration of services with a memorable elegance of form. They were projects in which 'structure and services and their relation to spatial organization play an overt role and do so in a very overt way'.[5] The clients were typically new-style industries producing chemicals, plastics and pharmaceuticals, generally in locations distant from the old centres of industry in the Midlands and North of England.

The Building Group

Before Arup Associates came into being in 1963, there was the Building Group, as it became known, effectively an architectural practice under the umbrella of Ove Arup & Partners. Ronald Hobbs (1923–2006) – christened Bob by Arup to avoid confusion with Jenkins – was an outstanding engineer who had briefly worked for the Royal Aircraft Establishment at Farnborough before joining Oscar Faber & Partners in 1945. He joined Arup in 1948 and took the lead in the development of the Building Group. He was close to Ove Arup and became one of the founding partners of Arup Associates, remaining a key figure in the practice until his retirement. Hobbs was the lead engineer, working with architects Easton & Robertson, for the Bank of England printing works in Loughton, Essex, completed in 1956 and notable for its vast (260m) printing hall, covered by a supremely elegant concrete vault. In an obituary, Jack Zunz recalled that 'Bob acted not only as an exceptionally gifted engineer, but also gave unobtrusive guidance, stimulated cohesion and team spirit which brought so much success and appreciation to the firm'. For Zunz, as for other colleagues, Hobbs had 'an aura, a ubiquitous presence, which created a feel-good factor amongst those around him'.[6]

It was Hobbs who recruited Derek Sugden to Arup after the two had worked together on buildings for Tate & Lyle in London Docks. Sugden (1924–2015) had begun his career as an apprentice in an engineering consultancy, studying part-time to qualify as an engineer at Westminster Technical College.

Ronald (Bob) Hobbs, who joined Arup in 1948, was instrumental in the development of the Building Group

The Bank of England Printing Works at Loughton, Essex, 1952–6 – Ronald Hobbs acted as lead engineer, working with architects Easton & Robertson

A young Derek Sugden in the foreman's office

The fourth of the founding partners of Arup Associates was Philip (later Sir Philip) Dowson (1924–2014). Born in South Africa, Dowson had studied at Clare College, Cambridge, after war service in the Royal Navy, before enrolling at the Architectural Association in London, 'a cockpit of passionate post-war ideology and debate, mostly centring around the work and social aims of Le Corbusier', as he later described it.[7] Dowson's final-year thesis at the AA on 'the problems of permanence' discussed issues of prefabrication and indus-trialised production, which were highly relevant to the ongoing programme of post-war reconstruction. Dowson's work came to the notice of Ove Arup through Ronald Jenkins, one of his tutors at the AA, and an interview was arranged. Dowson was initially taken on for a six-month period to work on the development of a prefabrication system for school building using timber and plywood. He began work in the Arup office in the autumn of 1953 with another young architect, Francis Pym (1924–2009), joining him to work on the pro-ject. A school for disabled children in Hertfordshire was completed in a few months, using the Arup system.

Early industrial buildings

But Dowson was soon fully occupied with commissions for industrial build-ings. He and Pym worked with Hobbs on the factory for Chemical Building Products in Hemel Hempstead (until Pym left to launch his own practice, where his best-known building was a major extension to the Ulster Museum).

Philip Dowson, the fourth founding partner of Arup Associates, joined the Arup office in 1953

Sugden, who had considerable experience of working on factory projects, was called in to assist with the steelwork design. 'It was the first real piece of architecture with which I was involved', Dowson recalled.[8] The *Architectural Review* commented that the building 'could be a turning-point in establishing an industrial vernacular for the small factory in Britain. Here for the first time are genuinely modern and mass-produced industrial forms – curtain walls and aluminium sheeting – used without applied "art" to give an elegant solution which arises directly from the functional needs'.[9]

Other such projects followed, three of them for CIBA at Duxford, near Cambridge, others for the American pharmaceutical company Smith Kline & French at Welwyn Garden City, which involved new laboratories as well as production spaces, for York Shipley at Basildon, and for the adhesives manufacturer Evode in Stafford. Sugden considered a factory as 'primarily a service package. Its success is wholly dependent on the way the environment is controlled and the way in which the factory services, as well as the environmental services, are controlled.'[10] A key element in the improved working environment that this new generation of industrial buildings offered was an ample supply of natural light.

As early as 1950, Arup had completed a factory at Duxford for Aero Research Ltd (later taken over by the Swiss company CIBA), extending a complex that had been developed there in the 1930s, where Aero Research's pioneering work on bonding adhesives had underpinned the development of the Mosquito,

Laboratories for Smith Kline & French in Welwyn Garden City, 1957–61 – the influence of Mies was clear

arguably the finest British aircraft of the Second World War. The project architect for the factory, working under Geoffrey Wood, was Barbara Priestley, a
graduate of the Architectural Association and daughter of the writer J B Priestley (who was a friend of Ove Arup). Innovative in many respects, for example
in the use of sheer glazed walls to enclose the production area, the building
was rigorously functional but perhaps lacked the aesthetic flair that Dowson, it
seems, injected into later CIBA commissions. These included the Araldite Plant
(1954–8), a laboratory block that was strongly Miesian in feel (1954–8), and a
multipurpose block, featuring slender canopied roofs of aluminium (1960–4).
Pevsner thought these buildings 'all extremely good and relaxed. Only the latest
building has the ambition to be dramatic', an adjective that did not signal his
approval.[11] Most of these buildings have now been demolished, though the 1950
factory survives remarkably intact. Demolition has also been the fate of most
of the other early Arup factory buildings.

Working on the laboratories for Smith Kline, a project Arup took over from
Leslie Martin, Sugden was sent to the USA for six weeks to make an intensive
study of new pharmaceutical laboratories, an example of how British designers
learned from America in the post-war period. Sugden admitted that he became
'obsessed by Mies' after his American tour. He saw the Seagram Building newly
finished and was 'bowled over' by it, while he was equally impressed by Skidmore,
Owings & Merrill's Lever House.[12] Sugden's American connections were later

Aero Research's Araldite Plant, Duxford, 1959

Laboratories and Process Building for Aero Research Ltd at Duxford, 1959

Multipurpose Building, CIBA (ARL) Ltd, Duxford, 1960–4

The Evode Factory in Stafford (1960–6), one
of a number of outstanding early works by the
Building Group that have since been demolished

cemented by teaching stints, extending over 20 years, at Pennsylvania State University, thanks to an initial invitation from Peter Shepheard when he was Dean of its Graduate School of Fine Arts. For Sugden, the early factory projects were a perfect marriage of architecture and engineering; too many recent factory buildings, he argued, were little more than 'visual slums'. He believed strongly that factories should be agreeable places to work as well as efficient centres of production – functional and attractive.

Dowson's aesthetic ambitions, which were to be realised in his later Oxford and Cambridge college projects, were evident, too, in the Smith Kline project and in the remarkably elegant, evenly day-lit, internal spaces of the York Shipley factory at Basildon, covered by a roof supported on slender steel columns and with triangulated beams providing ducts for services. The *Architects' Journal* described the roof system as 'a model example of integration'.[13] The influence of Mies was very much to the fore in the first of the series of factory buildings for Evode Ltd in Stafford, completed in 1962. Again the AJ was enthusiastic: 'almost every detail is a pleasure in itself', it commented. 'No junction, edge or corner has been left to chance ... Such meticulous detailing is rare'.[14] The Evode site is now occupied by off-the-peg warehouse sheds clad in corrugated steel, all the Arup buildings having been demolished.

The emergence of Arup Associates

One consequence of the highly favourable coverage that the Building Group's work received in the professional press was growing criticism from some of the architectural practices working in collaboration with Ove Arup & Partners, who saw an engineering firm muscling into their domain. Dowson, as an architect, was accused of undermining his own profession. For Sugden, it was a matter of architects wanting engineers kept in their place – 'the letters ARIBA stood for And Remember I'm the Bloody Architect', he joked. 'Ove challenged that sort of thinking.'[15] When Arup Associates formally emerged as an architectural practice in its own right, its multidisciplinary credentials were fundamental. The Smith Kline project, where the client – in line with American practice – declined to employ a quantity surveyor, led to Arup's signing up its first QS, Dennis Stone, in 1957. Dowson recalled:

> It was during this project that we realised that if Arup's were to be able to act in a fully professional way in the interests of our clients, we would need to have a wider spread of disciplines available in-house to pre-empt problems before they occurred. Our unsophisticated building industry was not yet equipped to handle these, particularly in the areas of mechanical engineering and environmental control, and we had to evolve in order to keep up and match the rapid developments in these fields.[16]

Arup's therefore expanded to include electrical and heating engineers among its specialist professionals. Max Fordham, who was to become a celebrated pioneer of environmentally benign services engineering, joined the Building Group in 1961, leaving to establish his own practice in 1968.

Dowson recalled that 'It was our work at Duxford that really put Arup's architecture on the map'.[17] Detailed reports of some of the factory projects in leading architectural journals fuelled further criticism that an engineering practice was undermining the architectural profession. When Dowson won a commission for new buildings for Oxford's Somerville College in 1958, the advent of Arup as a significant presence on the British architectural scene was confirmed. The first of three buildings at Somerville designed by Dowson – Margery Fry and Elizabeth Nuffield House – was completed in 1964, the same year that saw the completion of the George Thomson Building for Corpus Christi College, Cambridge. Dowson recalled that Arup's immediate reaction to the Somerville commission was 'that I should go into private practice, but by then my six months had already turned into nine years, relationships had been built up, and I believed profoundly in multi-disciplinary working'. The outcome was that the Building Group was reborn as Arup Associates in 1963 and, Dowson commented, 'in professional terms, we made "an honest woman" of ourselves'.[18]

Within a few years of the foundation of Arup Associates, there were four multidisciplinary groups, including architects, structural and services engineers, quantity surveyors, and other professionals. This strategy was rooted in the thinking of Ove Arup and was fundamental to the practice's success. The advantages for clients of dealing with one organisation were obvious. Group 1 focused on industrial buildings, the foundation on which the Building Group had flourished. Group 3, headed by Tim Sturgis (recruited to Arup in 1960), worked on university buildings and was the group with which Dowson worked most often. Group 4, led by John Brandenburger and John Hopkins, had a mixed workload, including residential projects. By the mid-1970s, there were seven groups, with more than 200 staff. But none matched the success of Group 2.

Peter Foggo and Group 2

Peter Foggo (1930–93), who became the fifth partner in Arup Associates in 1966, joined Arup in 1959 after a short stint with Architects' Co-Partnership. He had a profound influence on the direction of the practice's work, for his collaboration with the developer Stuart Lipton at Finsbury Avenue and Broadgate introduced Arup Associates to the world of speculative office design. Lipton describes him as being 'far and away the most talented architect I've ever worked with'.[19] For some years, Foggo combined his work at Arup Associates with private practice in partnership with David Thomas, a fellow graduate of the Liverpool School of Architecture. Together, they designed a series of innovative houses, of which the most distinctive is the Sorrell House at Bosham Hoe, near Chichester, completed in 1960. In 1968–9 they infilled a gap in a typical Pimlico street, the result of wartime bombing, to create two houses for themselves, stacked one above the other, with a lettable apartment below.

Foggo headed up Group 2 at Arup Associates, which Lipton describes as 'virtually an independent practice'. Other leading lights in the group, which typically never included more than three architects, were Les Winter, a design manager and administrator; Peter Skead, an outstanding engineer who had worked on Sydney Opera House; and Bruce Vickers, the lead quantity surveyor for the group. An inspiring leader, who instilled loyalty, and an unsparing critic when the need arose, Foggo 'ran his group like a fiefdom', according to Rab Bennetts, who joined Arup Associates in 1977 and worked with Foggo for eight years. Nicholas Hare, who came to the practice for his year out in 1969 and returned to work with Foggo, remembers the latter as a hugely practical designer who 'simply knew instinctively how to get things done'. Other partners were kept at arm's length. Foggo shunned personal publicity, however, which is one reason why his contribution to post-war British architecture has been seriously underestimated.

Peter Foggo, who became a partner in the practice in 1966

The Sorrell House, Sussex, designed by Peter Foggo and David Thomas, built in 1960

The Horizon Factory

In 1968, Foggo's team began work on an industrial building of truly monumental scale. The client for the Horizon Factory in Nottingham was John Player & Sons, part of the Imperial Tobacco Group. Tobacco had long been one of the foundations of a local economy based on 'Boots, bikes and baccy', and the city already boasted some outstanding examples of industrial architecture, notably the buildings designed in the 1930s by Sir Owen Williams for the Boots Pure Drug Company.

The structural engineer Tony Taylor, who joined Ove Arup & Partners in 1967 from the contractor McAlpine and subsequently moved to Group 2 in Arup Associates, had a key role in the 19-member team for the Nottingham project and thereafter worked regularly with Foggo. The first major hurdle to be tackled was that of site clearance. The site for the factory, on the Lenton Industrial Estate, had been used as a refuse dump and was heavily polluted. It had to be drained and opened up to diffuse dangerous concentrations of methane gas, and Professor Alan Gemmell of Keele University (who was well known as a panel member of BBC Radio's *Gardeners' Question Time* team) advised on the new landscape. The foundations for the factory took the form of piles driven deep into the underlying sandstone. Piling completed, work on the superstructure began in autumn 1969. The building was handed over two years later, the fast-track programme a consequence of the construction strategy devised by Peter Skead using repetitive components, for example in the formation of the ribbed-concrete floor system. This provided a model that was to be used with dramatic effect more than a decade later for the Finsbury Avenue and Broadgate office projects, on which Skead again worked with Foggo.

The brief at Nottingham was for a very large (125,000m^2) building in which flexibility and adaptability were central concerns. Ironically, this cathedral of cigarette production was commissioned just as the link between smoking and lung cancer and other diseases was becoming well established and a question mark already hung over the future of the tobacco industry in Britain, which employed more than 7,000 people in Nottingham alone. The potential for conversion of the building to another use was one factor in the project's design. The Horizon Factory was nevertheless built for a long life, its massive *in situ* concrete structure designed to take very heavy floor loadings, with 30m^2 column-free spaces providing the element of flexibility demanded by the brief. The vast (45,000m^2) production area is sandwiched between a 6m-deep roof space, housing air conditioning, lighting and sprinklers, and a storey-height void supplying power and water, which also serves a subsidiary production area at ground level. The ground floor also accommodated car parking, a packing and despatch area accessed directly by trucks, and the massive power plant fuelled by North Sea gas, its first large-scale use in an industrial building. The waste heat recovery system was equally innovative. A large restaurant, bank, medical centre and other facilities were provided for the 2,000 staff working in the building.

The Horizon Factory, Nottingham

Horizon Factory: interior

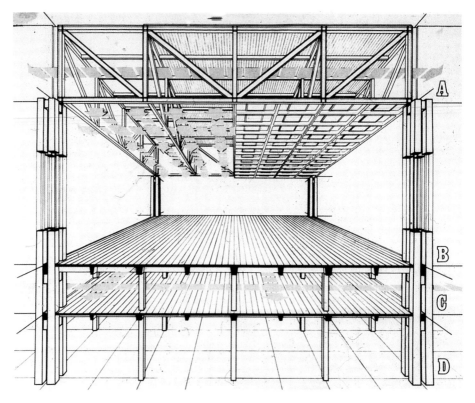

Horizon Factory: section, showing integration of structure and services

The services strategy was a major driver for the whole project. Tobacco was, then as now, a heavily taxed commodity; at the time of the commission, John Player were paying a staggering £1.25 million a day in duty, levied on the raw material before manufacture. In the new building, tobacco dust left over from the production process was collected, weighed and valued by the excise officers and prepaid tax could be reclaimed. Control of the moisture in the tobacco was also vital and was achieved via air conditioning and controlled humidity, with extractor fans collecting waste tobacco.

Architecturally dramatic (Miesian in its inspiration) and technically innovative, the Horizon Factory could be seen as embodying Ove Arup's ideal of 'total design'. But the collaborative process driving the project extended beyond Arup Associates' own team of architects, engineers and surveyors to a pioneering use of a management contract, devised by Foggo and Vickers, operated by Bovis Ltd, with construction work subcontracted, and involving a partnership of architect, client and contractor, Player's having set up their own team to work on the project. The *Architectural Review* declared the factory a contradiction:

Horizon Factory: interior of plant room

It is highly specialised yet suitable for any manufacturing purpose ... Its importance lies in the integration and scale of the thinking. It was designed as a heat engine, as a membrane to protect a delicate process, and as an un-conceited structure. It was assembled from identical sub-units each the size of an ordinary factory. Its architects worked inside the design team instead of following the ancient tradition of trying to lead it from over the horizon.[20]

The factory closed in May 2016, after an application for its statutory listing was rejected in 2015, and demolition is its likely fate.

The Trebor Factory

The Colchester factory designed by the Foggo team for Trebor Ltd, completed in 1980, was very different in terms of its brief and the particular technical problems the project posed. One issue was the fact that sugar, the basic raw material for Trebor's confectionery, has a corrosive effect on exposed concrete. Instead of a single huge production area, the factory was planned as two production areas linked by an internal street and with a warehouse and boiler house and the offices

Trebor Factory, Colchester, 1977–80

and amenity spaces placed centrally. Trebor was noted as a progressive employer, with a commitment to good working conditions for its staff, so ample daylight and views out to landscaped courtyards were a feature of the factory areas. The client's vision was of a working 'village', though David Thurlow, writing in the *Architects' Journal*, felt that this had been only partially realised – 'good villages evolve over years of growth and change, not from management handbooks'.[21] The architecture combined immaculate Miesian detailing with pyramidal roofs covered in concrete tiles. The use of steelwork, painted bright red, and extensive glazing for the plant room contrasted with the brick cladding of the production areas. The factory, closed after Trebor was taken over by Cadbury Schweppes in 1989, has now been successfully converted to house a series of small business units.

The diagram of the Trebor factory as a series of pavilions under pyramidal roofs has parallels with that of office projects by the practice, including that for CEGB in Bristol and, more particularly, Lloyd's of London at Chatham. Equally, there is a close relationship between the Horizon Factory and an educational project such as the Metallurgy and Materials Building at Birmingham University. All this underlines the seamlessness of the practice's work, equally enriched by the different emphases developed by its leaders under the group system.

Building projects for IBM

The foundation of Arup Associates opened the way for the new practice to win commissions for university buildings, offices and public and cultural buildings and to compete for work internationally. Its expertise in the design of factory and research buildings was well tuned to the needs of the new industries emerging in post-war Britain, still in the 1950s a smoky land of textile mills, coal mines and steam trains. When Harold Wilson's Labour Government was elected in 1964 it declared itself committed to promoting 'the white heat of technology'. Arup Associates was well equipped to create buildings for a new industry that was to transform the global economy.

When the American computer giant IBM decided to develop major research and production facilities in Britain, it opted for a site at Havant, near Portsmouth, and acquired further land from the Royal Navy nearby at North Harbour, Cosham. Between 1966 and 1982, phased development on the two sites was undertaken by Arup Associates. At Havant, the Computer Centre (completed in 1969) and the 97,500m^2 Assembly Plant, completed in three construction phases in 1974, with a later (1978–9) extension, dwarfed the earlier Arup factory projects. The large Distribution Centre was constructed in two phases in 1968–72. The huge single-storey steel-framed buildings were clad in panels of white precast concrete, subdivided into fire compartments by service cores running at right angles to the main spine. A raised floor accommodated services.

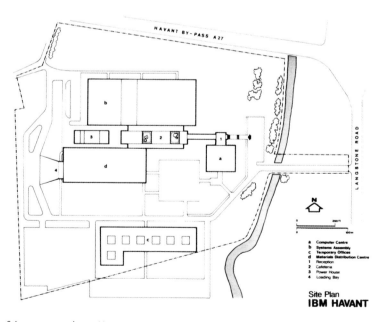

Plan of the IBM complex at Havant

IBM Computer Centre and Assembly Plant, Havant, 1969–71

At North Harbour, on land largely reclaimed from the sea, the Group 6 team led by David Thomas (who joined the Building Group in 1958 and left Group 2 to head up the IBM work) and including Alistair Gourlay and Stuart Mercer, was responsible for several phases of development, following on from the 1970 master plan. The first office building on the site was completed in two phases of construction in 1975, with a computer centre, the third phase of development at Cosham, completed two years later. The most impressive element of the IBM complex at North Harbour was, however, the 34,000m² UK headquarters building, commissioned in 1977 and constructed between 1978 and 1982, on a site between two earlier buildings, with office space in a series of four stepped pavilions linked by a two-level steel and glass barrel-vaulted arcade incorporating shops, an exhibition centre and an auditorium. A glazed entrance pavilion formed the reception area for the whole site. One of the blocks accommodated a staff restaurant seating 1,000, broken down across a series of levels, stepping down to an open terrace with waterfront views. Landscaping and planting to designs by James Russell provided an appropriate setting for this prestigious development. Breaking with the aesthetic of the earlier office buildings at Cosham – solid, concrete-framed blocks – this final phase of development, completed in 1982 by Group 3, reflected the rise of High Tech as a dominant theme in British architecture. The working relationship between architect and client was particularly harmonious, IBM praising Arup Associates' 'tenacity and ingenuity' and its capacity for teamwork. IBM withdrew from the Havant site in 1994 and has vacated some of the buildings at Cosham, but buildings on both sites have adapted well to alternative use.

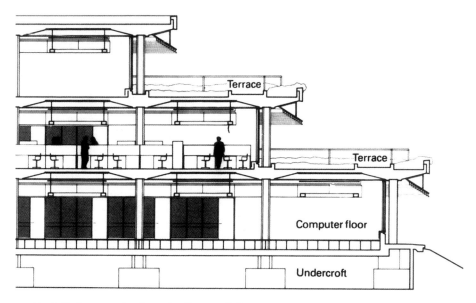

IBM North Harbour: section through offices, 1978–82

IBM North Harbour, Cosham, 1978–82

Internal Courtyard, Office Building, Cosham, 1978–9

Portsmouth projects

From 1970 onwards, Arup Associates was responsible for a series of buildings for the Royal Navy's base at Portsmouth. The dockyard has a history extending back to Tudor times and was the Navy's principal seat of operations, a place where ships were built and maintained, and an industrial site on a very large scale. The architect Dave King, who joined Group 1 in 1970 after a stint in Denys Lasdun's office, was soon thrown into the Portsmouth project when Brian Carter, already working on it, quit to pursue an academic career in the USA. Over the next decade, working with structural engineer Charlie Wymer, he oversaw four phases of construction at the dockyard. The first involved the replacement of the Boiler Shop East, a decrepit 19th-century building. The initial plan was to repair it, but the building was found to be in parlous condition and was replaced by the most important of the new Arup buildings, the Heavy Plate Shop. The 150m-long building had to accommodate three traditionally independent shipyard trades – boilermakers, shipwrights and smiths – with a battery of heavy machinery. It was constructed on a steel frame on a 12m × 24m grid, with a massive concrete floor slab. External walls were clad with red-brick cavity-infill panels. In the best Arup Associates tradition, electrical and mechanical services were integrated into the structure, with service runs left visible and accessible. Critic Adrian Gale admired the precise detailing, 'in proportion with the scale of the building so that its sheer size never becomes overbearing, either inside or out'.[22] The use of bold colour was a welcome feature of the internal space, with the structural steel painted red, cranes yellow and machinery blue. Gale concluded that this was 'the first building to be constructed within the dockyard for many years that matches the pedigree of the distinguished eighteenth century forebears'.[23]

Following on from the Heavy Plate Shop, Arup Associates' team was commissioned to design a development adjacent to the dry docks at No. 3 Basin. These support buildings serving the crews of ships undergoing repair and maintenance were 'so much like ships ... we followed "ship architecture" slavishly. The logic was inexorable – a thin building serving a ship on either side was really just a landbound vessel'.[24] Next came a commission for a three-storey office block, with workshops at ground-floor level. A significant issue here was that of noise: a 900mm air gap served to exclude the impact of pneumatic hammers operating close to the building and was cleverly used as part of a heat-reclamation system using low-pressure plenum ducts. An 'air-slab' roof system pioneered in Arup Associates' additions to Truman's Brewery in London, used an in situ coffered slab as an extract plenum to draw air over light fittings and provide cooling at source.

The last of the new dockyard buildings, the PAS Building, was designed to service the port auxiliary boats that ferried Royal Navy and dockyard staff around the port. The big industrial shed, for this was what it was, incorporated

The Heavy Plate Shop, the most important of a number of buildings by the practice at the naval base in Portsmouth (1971–9)

a lift to haul the vessels out of the water. A listed clock tower had to be accommodated in the scheme. Dave King left Arup Associates in 1977 and was later a co-founder of the practice Shed KM, but working at Portsmouth rekindled his interest in sailing and he has a house close to the dockyard.

Conclusion

Industrial buildings formed the foundation for the Building Group a decade before Arup Associates achieved its separate identity within the Arup empire. The multidisciplinary approach generated an innovative response to the needs of industry that made the practice a leader in the field. Arup Associates was important in driving the process of technical innovation within the practice and remained a significant element in its workload into the 21st century, as shown by the 185,000m² Jaguar Land Rover engine plant at Wolverhampton.

2 University buildings

Writing to a fellow academic in September 1966, Dame Janet Vaughan, Principal of Somerville College, Oxford, recalled the circumstances that led to Philip Dowson's appointment in 1958 as architect for the College's new buildings. Dowson's name had been put forward by the eminent scientist and fellow of Somerville, Dorothy Hodgkin. 'Dorothy told the Governing Body that there was somebody who had built a very nice bus shelter in her village. I think at that time he had built nothing else! He came to see the Governing Body because we all respect Dorothy's judgement. We took him on ...'.[1]

Dowson's wartime service in the Royal Navy had been dramatically curtailed when, aboard the destroyer HMS *Ursa* in the Pacific a week after VE Day, he was diagnosed with advanced tuberculosis. He spent 15 months in a military hospital in Australia. On his repatriation to England, Dowson was sent to a sanatorium at Mundesley in Norfolk, in the same county as his family home in the village of Geldeston. He was able to visit his parents, but within weeks of his return to Norfolk, his father, Robert Manning Dowson, died of cancer. He is commemorated by a tablet in the bus shelter attached to the Wherry Inn, a modest structure that was Philip Dowson's first completed building.

Above: The bus shelter at Geldeston, Norfolk, was Philip Dowson's first built work, late 1940s
Opposite: Margery Fry- Elisabeth Nuffield House for graduates, 1961–4
Overleaf: Vaughan House, Somerville College, Oxford, completed in 1966

Restored to health, Dowson went up to Clare College, Cambridge, in the autumn of 1946. As a schoolboy at Gresham's in Norfolk, he had been attracted by the idea of becoming an architect after discovering the *Architectural Review*: 'it was there that I first saw, as a fifteen year old, the beautiful work of Le Corbusier and Max Fry'.[2] From Clare, he went on to the Architectural Association to complete his diploma, and thence to Ove Arup & Partners.

Buildings for Somerville College, Oxford

Somerville College was founded in 1879, the second Oxford institution catering for women students, although it achieved full college status within the University only in 1960. Janet Vaughan, who had pursued a distinguished career as a medical researcher during the 1930s, became Principal in 1945, retiring in 1967.

Not the least of Vaughan's achievements was the development of an emergency diet that saved the lives of thousands of starving inmates in the liberated Belsen concentration camp. The College's first post-war architectural commissions went to Paul Geddes Hyslop (1899–1988), an architect whose pre-war career had included the extensive remodelling of Buscot Park for Lord Faringdon, and who had already designed a residential block for King's College, Cambridge, in 1950. For Somerville, Hyslop designed a residential building, also completed in 1950, and an extension to the library, in 1956. The residential accommodation was carried out in 'a smart if nonetheless unadventurous neo-Georgian style' and the library in a Festival of Britain idiom, both of which seemed reactionary to progressive critics, although Alistair Fair has commented that his work 'nodded to the language and materials of architectural modernity, but not in an alarming way'.[3]

'The first buildings at Oxford in the language of the C20', Pevsner wrote, were 'the intelligently planned group of polygons' generally known as the Beehive Building at St John's College, built in 1958–60 to designs by the Architects' Co-Partnership.[4] The project was the first of a new generation of college buildings reflecting the triumph of modernism over the traditionalists. Dowson's appointment at Somerville can be seen as part of that process. Vaughan's first priority was to provide accommodation in college for the growing number of graduate students, who generally had to find lodgings in the city. She was reputedly spurred on by a visit to a Nepalese graduate whom she found sick in the damp chill of an Oxford winter and living in squalid conditions.

Dowson made his first presentation to the College in November 1958, and designs for a site fronting Little Clarendon Street were worked up during the following year. At a meeting of the College Building Committee in February 1959, Dowson argued against the use of brick as used by Hyslop. Brick, he insisted, would be 'wrong for so high a building. Concrete would be most satisfactory. It was the cheapest material, and it could be made to look very attractive.'[5] In May of the same year, it was finally resolved that rooms in both buildings would be accessed via corridors, rather than the more traditional Oxford arrangement of staircases originally proposed.[6] The two blocks would be raised on a podium, with parking beneath and shops on the street frontage, the graduate building being located on the line of Little Clarendon Street and the undergraduate accommodation set back. Somerville was not a rich college, and money for the two buildings had to be raised. A fundraising meeting at the House of Commons in 1960 was attended by a number of alumnae, including Margaret Thatcher MP and Vera Brittain, whose daughter Shirley Williams was another distinguished alumna. By 1962, with the first of the two buildings set to go on site, the budget for the two buildings had risen to £275,000. Margery Fry and Elizabeth Nuffield House – named after the college's Principal from 1926 to 1931 (Fry) and an important proponent of education for women (Nuffield) – was opened in October 1964. Vaughan House, with 60 undergraduate rooms rather than the 48 originally planned, thanks to the addition of an extra floor, was completed two years later.

From 1960 onwards, Dowson was assisted at Somerville by Tim Sturgis, who had been at the AA with him and joined the Building Group in the same year. A young David Levitt assisted with the detailing of Vaughan House, while Ron Marsh acted as project engineer under Derek Sugden. The defining feature of both buildings was the use of an external precast concrete frame, with the largely glazed walls set back behind it. 'The example of Gothic stone buildings, with their single material for all elements, and their slim window mullions, grooved for glazing, moulded to catch the light, were an inspiration', says Sturgis.[7] Praised by Pevsner, the buildings received a cooler reception from the *Architectural Review*, where the critic Nicholas Taylor detected in Margery Fry House 'too many signs of that imposition of artistic effect that has distorted recent Oxbridge buildings'.[8]

For the modern-minded student editors of *New Oxford*, welcoming the 'ambitious and fascinating scheme', Dowson's appointment was to be applauded: 'Somerville has done well to introduce him to Oxford'.[9] The scheme also relates well to Little Clarendon Street, continuing the line of small, specialised shops and restaurants, while Margery Fry House adds an urban scale.

The Fry and Vaughan buildings were followed by a further commission from Somerville: the Wolfson Building, completed in 1967, occupies a prominent site backing on to Walton Street. The project further developed the integration of the structural frame and external wall by introducing projecting bay windows, with window seats formed of precast concrete and a large front pane pushed through the structural frame, with small opening lights to the side. The Building Committee this time included students, and Dowson noted that their priorities included 'variety, allowance for self-expression, and the need to plan against loneliness'.[10] It was also a personal response to large windows. 'I couldn't bear being in a building that was like a piece of card with a hole cut in it', he told Elain Harwood. 'I liked the relationship between inside and out, with little balconies or oriels where people could sleep. With such aedicules, you have a part of your inside world on the outside.'[11] The building has an expressive quality that makes it a striking presence on the street. Pevsner thought it a little too expressive, coining the phrase 'brutalism among the ladies' to describe its impact.[12] With the completion of this building, Janet Vaughan's transformation of the college was complete.

Wolfson Building, Somerville College, Oxford

Interior of student room in the Wolfson Building, showing seat placed in projecting window bay

George Thomson Building, Corpus Christi College, Cambridge

Meanwhile, Dowson and his team had completed Arup Associates' first commission in Cambridge. The George Thomson Building, constructed in 1961–4 for Corpus Christi College, was set in the extensive grounds of the Victorian Leckhampton House, well removed from the main college site across the River Cam. With student numbers rising, Corpus had been considering constructing a new residential building on land it owned across Bene't Street, but the project went into limbo and the site is now occupied by the 1990s Robert Bedlam Building, designed by Nicholas Hare (himself a former member of Arup Associates). Instead, the College decided to establish a residential base solely for graduates on the Leckhampton site. The search for a suitable architect began, and in July 1961, a party from Corpus Christi visited a number of new college buildings in Oxford. Powell & Moya and Denys Lasdun were approached as potential candidates for the commission after Chamberlin, Powell & Bon, Hugh Casson and David Roberts were ruled out, but both practices declined on account of pressure of work. Leslie Martin, then head of Cambridge University's Department of Architecture, was approached for advice – a capacity in which he acted for a considerable number of higher education projects across Britain. Martin recommended Dowson as one possible contender, along with Trevor Dannatt, Peter Moro and Leonard Manasseh. The final choice was between Dannatt and Dowson, and the latter was eventually appointed. It was reported with approval that he was 'deeply interested in the interior arrangements of residences for graduates or undergraduates'.[13]

Dowson and Sugden came to Cambridge to discuss a variety of options for the building. One, with rooms around a series of courtyards, would have involved the loss of a number of mature trees, something firmly resisted by a number of senior members of the College. The plan evolved into two pavilions constructed within the former kitchen garden, four and five storeys high respectively, with stairs and service rooms (kitchens and shared bathrooms) in a link block that also housed services in its wall cavities. Every room was given a garden view, with sliding windows (later sealed on health and safety grounds) allowing residents to enjoy fresh air and to connect with the landscape. The external structural frame of precast concrete – the defining feature of the pavilions – was a development of that used at Somerville, but construction was simplified by the use of storey-height prefabricated H-frames, producing an exoskeleton with, as at Somerville, the external wall of the building set back behind the frame. The linking service block was clad in brick, and the diagram of the building could be seen as an early British example of the separation of 'served' and 'servant' spaces, a strategy that had been developed slightly earlier in the work of the American master Louis Kahn. Tim Sturgis recalls that 'the intention was that each material used should express its own character: the bonyness of concrete, the earthiness of the brick, the tautness of the steel window frames'.[14]

Above: George Thomson Building, Corpus Christi College, Cambridge, 1961–4

Overleaf: Exterior of Sir Thomas White Building, 1970–6: the most ambitious of Philip Dowson's Oxbridge projects

The building received a highly favourable critical response. Writing even before its completion, the editors of *Cambridge New Architecture* pronounced it 'clearly one of Cambridge's best post-war buildings in every way: planning, structure, economy and social sensibility'. The building showed 'a real understanding of student sociology in its grouping of rooms around the service areas ... it provides for fully adult scholars and not just undergraduates in BA gowns'.[15] The most admired critic of the day, Reyner Banham, described the building as 'a pretty little out-college'. Banham had little good to say for most recent Cambridge architecture, considering it 'effete' and full of 'self-cancelling vacuity'. The only 1960s building he admired unreservedly was James Stirling's History Faculty Library. But, he wrote, 'the History Faculty is not quite alone in kicking the pretences. Leckhampton does it too, but it does it so prettily and in such total seclusion that no gesture is made'.[16] The George Thomson Building was instantly popular with its residents, too: PhD researchers appreciated the calm of the site and its detachment from the rest of the college. Half a century on, the beauty of the site, insulated from the tides of tourists and shoppers crowding the city centre, is beguiling and the architecture is in total harmony with the landscape. Rooms there remain oversubscribed.[17]

The St John's College, Oxford, project

Dowson returned to Oxford to design the most costly and ambitious of his Oxbridge college projects, for St John's College. The college has been noted for its pioneering patronage of the Architects' Co-Partnership (ACP) thanks to the architectural historian and fellow of the college, Howard Colvin, a potent factor in the appointment. St John's had become wealthy with the development of its landholdings in North Oxford in the 19th century, and in the mid-1960s, it resolved to undertake a major expansion project for which it was prepared to allot up to £1 million. A key aim was to allow students to live in college, if they wished, for the whole of their time at Oxford. Greater provision had also to be made for the growing number of graduate students, and, unlike Somerville and Corpus, St John's had both money and land. Beyond the North Quad, the site of ACP's Beehive Building, an area occupied by gardens and squash courts, extended through to Museum Road (leading to the Victorian University Museum), where a number of Victorian houses were in college ownership and used partly as graduate accommodation. The then bursar, Arthur Garrard, put forward a plan to develop this area. Breaking out of the enclosure of its historic quadrangles, he argued, would give the college the opportunity to evolve as 'a mixed community with houses for tutors, accommodation for married and single graduates with their social centre, college administrative offices etc.'[18]

Garrard's progressive vision was eventually taken up by the College when a New Building Committee was appointed in 1966, with Howard Colvin as a member. Three architectural practices were approached for their ideas: Powell & Moya, William Whitfield, and, naturally, ACP. Powell & Moya declined to compete on the grounds that they were fully occupied with other projects, including the new Wolfson College at Oxford, exclusively for graduates, so the shortlist was expanded to include Howell Killick Partridge & Amis (HKPA, then completing buildings for St Anne's College) and Arup Associates.

The brief was for a very large development, including not only residential accommodation for undergraduates and graduates but also a lecture theatre, graduate common room, a new science library and car parking. A new dining room and possibly a swimming pool were also seen as desirable additions to the brief. Whitfield, ACP and HKPA were all ruled out, the latter's proposals being dismissed as 'crude and repetitive' while Whitfield's were seen as simply 'out of character'.[19] On 23 June 1967, the Governing Body voted to appoint Philip Dowson of Arup Associates to develop his proposals, subsequently resolving to 'let Mr Dowson have a free hand in designing the buildings'.[20] The college's mood was expansive, and around £700,000 was budgeted for the development. But within months, it became apparent that that estimate would be greatly exceeded: the College's new bursar, Harry Kidd, reckoned on a final cost of £1.15 million. St John's was wealthy, but there were worries that the project was getting out of control. Efforts were made to trim the brief by omitting the science library and swimming pool.

Dowson's winning proposal, designed with a team that included Alistair Gourlay and Richard Frewer, was for a development that, like Powell & Moya's much-admired Cripps Building at St John's College, Cambridge, cast aside the traditional Oxbridge quadrangle model in favour of a linear progression of blocks extending northwards to Museum Road. The scheme could be adapted, it was decided, to allow for construction in two phases, the first to be completed in 1972. By now, the estimated cost of the whole project was reckoned to be in excess of £1.7 million, and rising. In October 1969, a special meeting of fellows voted to totally abandon the northern element of the development, which would have involved the demolition of the Museum Road houses, while a major policy shift by the local authority ruled out the provision of parking on the site.

Writing many years later, Dowson blamed the rising cost of the scheme on the College: 'we were given an expanding and more complex brief by the governing body, which I believed to be indulgent and unnecessary'.[21] Within the College, Dowson was blamed by many – not least Kidd, whose relationship with the architect was chilly – for the rising budget, though no clear cost limit had ever been set. In August 1971, Kidd wrote that: 'I am inclined to fear that it is apt to be Philip's absence in South Africa, Mauritius, or wherever it may be that prevents inspiration from striking him on our behalf'.[22] The scene seemed set, perhaps, for a parting of the ways between architect and client. The evolution of a new scheme for what became the Sir Thomas White Building owed more than a little to the College's new President, the medieval historian Professor R W (later Sir Richard) Southern, with whom Dowson developed an amicable working relationship.

Tim Sturgis, a veteran of the Somerville and Corpus projects who was brought in to work on the new scheme, recalls that Dowson was always 'emotionally much involved' in the Oxbridge projects: 'he loved to participate in the talk at high table'.[23] Dowson admired Southern's 'gentle humour and old world courtesy', but the latter could also be critical. In December 1971, he wrote that 'if we continue to negotiate we must expect Dowson to continue to press his point of view and whatever evidence he produces will be slanted in the direction which he wishes to take. In the end, we shall have to agree with him out of sheer weariness or oppose him on grounds which are already well known.'[24] Southern visited the George Thomson Building in Cambridge and was apparently impressed. He also saw Denys Lasdun's recent building for Christ's College on the same visit and was left with an 'unpleasing impression',

Sir Thomas White Building: interior of student room showing bespoke furniture and sliding screens to windows

not least because Lasdun had used tinted glazing to baffle sunlight and increase the sense of privacy. Southern wrote to Dowson: 'my own feeling would be that the tinted glass is a solution to the problem of privacy but not a tolerable one. If the use of clear glass carries with it the need for the outer concrete structure I should certainly prefer the kind of arrangement which exists in the Corpus building'.[25] Arup Associates' new scheme, unveiled in December 1971, proposed an L-shaped development of 156 student rooms and sets housed in a series of 11 pavilions linked by service blocks and connected by a colonnaded cloister at ground-floor level. There were issues of detail to be resolved: tinted glazing, though favoured by Dowson, was firmly ruled out in favour of curtains, and hessian wall covering was vetoed in favour of plain plaster.

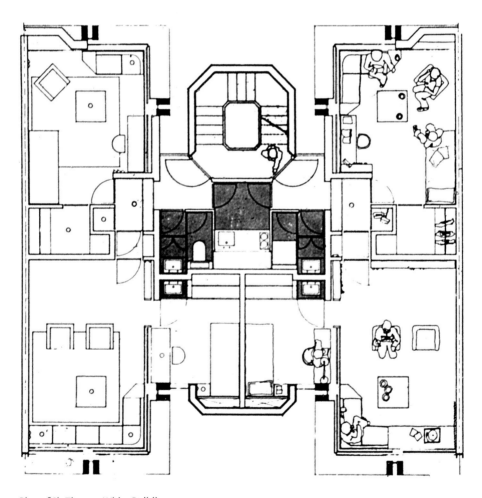

Plan of Sir Thomas White Building

But the scheme was given the go-ahead, and construction began in autumn 1972. The building was formally opened in June 1975, though some rooms had been occupied since the previous autumn.

The wealth of St John's, as compared to penurious Somerville, was reflected in the use of limestone as a cladding for the service towers containing stairs, bathrooms and kitchens and linking the residential pavilions in a reiteration of the Corpus diagram. There was also high-quality built-in furniture made by the firm of Gordon Russell. The landscape around the building and its relationship to its neighbours were also carefully considered, notably on Museum Road, where the new building straddled a carefully preserved stone wall. For Sturgis, 'this was the most assured and convincing of all the schemes for student rooms, the culmination of a long learning process. It seemed to incorporate both how to build with an exposed pre-cast concrete structure and how students wanted to live'.[26] The *Architectural Review* wrote approvingly of the building, but criticised a certain 'over-elaboration of structure'. The concrete frame 'is just a little overpowering'.[27]

The external concrete frame was also the key feature of Dowson's residential buildings for University College, Oxford, and Trinity Hall, Cambridge. But the St John's project was the most fully developed solution to the dilemma of the student room – 'a place of work and sleep, a retreat and a place to entertain, a place of privacy yet identifiably part of a larger community', as Dowson described it. 'How to reconcile these, and create at once somewhere with a sense of generosity and space'.[28] For Dowson, the St John's project reflected 'a wish to develop a relationship between the small scale and the large, and between the man-made and the natural via the intermediate spaces created between the interior and the exterior .... The combination of the scale of this scheme and the complexity of its brief, with the extreme vulnerability of its site, presented the most difficult architectural problem we have ever had to undertake.'[29]

For Michael Brawne, the 'very deliberate outlining of a space' seen in the college projects was 'very much a preoccupation of its designers and, one suspects, a reaction to the notions of anonymity and an unstated degree of flexibility which has bedeviled so much of present-day architecture'. The same agenda, 'creating a sense of belonging', could, he noted, be seen in Arup Associates' office projects of the 1970s (*see* Chapter 3).[30] The idea of the exoskeleton, with its offer of privacy and protection from the climate, was potentially applicable to housing projects beyond the universities. The post-war social housing boom largely bypassed Arup Associates, but its one substantial venture into the sector, the 18-storey Point Royal residential tower in the new town of Bracknell of 1959–64, also made effective use of an external structural frame.

Point Royal, Bracknell (1959–64): a rare social housing project by the practice

Buildings for the University of Birmingham

Oxbridge college projects became a much-admired aspect of Arup Associates' oeuvre, but the practice also played its part in the wider expansion of higher education in post-war Britain. In 1962, with the Fry Building in Oxford starting construction, Arup's Building Group was commissioned to design a major building for the University of Birmingham, to house the Departments of Metallurgy and Minerals Engineering. The site was on the University's Edgbaston campus, developed from 1900 onwards with an imposing range of neo-Byzantine buildings by Aston Webb as its defining feature. The University had commissioned a development plan from Casson & Conder in 1956 and buildings by that practice, HKPA and Chamberlin, Powell & Bon marked Birmingham's conversion to the cause of modernism. The Metallurgy and Minerals Building was designed to be built in three phases, with four separate blocks linked by a covered walkway at ground level. This was intended to form part of a series of covered walkways across the campus, an idea later abandoned. Laboratories with heavy equipment were located at ground-floor level, along with lecture theatres. The first floor housed other teaching spaces as well as offices for academic and administrative staff, while the top floor was occupied by specialist laboratories and research facilities for graduate students.

Metallurgy and Minerals Building, University of Birmingham: view of the interior shortly after completion

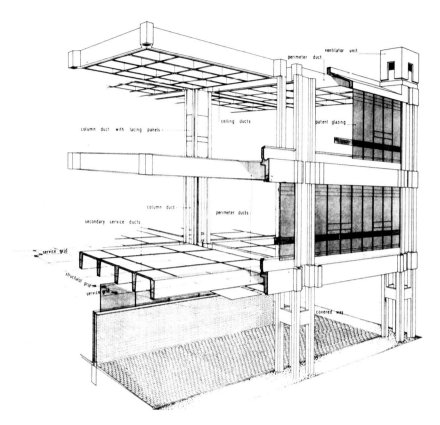

Metallurgy and Minerals Building, showing the 'tartan grid' integrating services and structure

The project capitalised on the Building Group's experience of designing economical and flexible industrial buildings. Bob Hobbs oversaw the structural design, with Max Fordham working on services. The main structure of the building was entirely of precast concrete, with only main floor and roof slabs cast on site. A group of four columns where the corners of the 20ft (6m) square floor plates meet provides space for services and ventilation ducts, expressed externally by extracting roof vents at the top of the column clusters. Services are routed horizontally along 3ft (0.9m) interstices between the floor plates. The architectural expression of the building is rigorously rational, with the bays between the service runs filled with low-cost patent glazing and opening louvres. Spaces requiring mechanical ventilation were concentrated at the centre of the blocks, where non-structural internal partitions were of white brick, with recessed joints. Self-supporting staircases were framed by minimal steel hand-rails. The fundamentally functional nature of the building notwithstanding, its interiors reflected a sure aesthetic sense – the hand of Philip Dowson was everywhere apparent. But the particular significance of the building lies in its

Minerals and Physical Metallurgy Building, University of Birmingham: general view of the exterior

servicing strategy: this was the first use of the 'tartan grid', integrating structure and services and a fundamental feature of a number of subsequent Arup
Associates projects.

The Metallurgy and Minerals Building was listed as long ago as 1993. A sensitive refurbishment completed in 2013 by Associated Architects saw significant
changes to its internal configuration, with new laboratories, write-up spaces
and seminar rooms linked by internal streets, which connect all four blocks.
The original glazing was replaced with a new system matching the appearance
of the original but with a greatly improved environmental performance; Dowson came to visit and approved, it seems.

Arup Associates was responsible for several other buildings on the Birmingham campus, most notably the 13-storey Muirhead Tower (1964–70), which
features a juxtaposition of 'dark' floors without windows containing lecture
theatres with 'light' floors for tutorial rooms and offices. The tower has been
described as 'Birmingham University's most controversial building, and the
most mannered in Arup Associates' work', and as 'variously loved or loathed'.[31]

Muirhead Tower, housing the Faculty of Arts, University of Birmingham, 1964–70

Above: Nuclear Physics Building, University of Oxford, 1959–69
Opposite: The Attenborough Building, University of Leicester, 1964–70

Other university projects

The tartan grid was a defining feature of Arup Associates' work at Loughborough University, which began with a master plan commissioned in 1964 and
was the first project to be developed by a team from Group 2 led by Peter Foggo
and David Thomas. The campus was conceived as a grid of buildings and inter-
stitial spaces. The principal focus of the university was scientific and technical,
so the laboratory buildings designed by the practice shared the industrial character of the Birmingham Metallurgy and Minerals Building. Michael Brawne
was doubtful about the wisdom of applying the tartan grid to an entire campus,
including residential buildings: 'modular rigour has undoubtedly an allure of
consistency but this can often get in the way of genuinely rational planning'.[32]
Other university projects included the Attenborough Building for the University
of Leicester and buildings for the Universities of Sheffield and Surrey, the latter
a new campus on a green site close to Guildford Cathedral.

Arup's Building Group experience in designing modern laboratories led to
commissions from both Oxford and Cambridge universities. The Nuclear Physics
Building forming part of the 'Keble Road Triangle' in Oxford was completed in
1970. Geoffrey Tyack considered it 'an ungainly pile … notable mainly for the
extraordinary fan-shaped concrete superstructure to the Van der Graaf generator
(a kind of linear accelerator) which greets the visitor approaching the centre of
Oxford along the Banbury Road'.[33] The Engineering and Metallurgy Building,
completed in 1976, Tyack described as having 'an air of intimidating power …
the massive complex bears no relationship to the streets around it'.[34]

In Cambridge, Arup Associates took over the redevelopment of the New
Museums Site from Denys Lasdun after his 1960 proposal for a series of towers
there, one 190ft (58m) high, had caused some outrage. Three departments –
Zoology, Metallurgy and Computer Science – were to be housed in the new
development, effectively in one large building, completed in 1971, in place of
the comprehensive redevelopment proposed by Lasdun. Sugden recalled that
'we were thrown into the world of academic infighting – the departments were
competing for the lion's share of space on the site'.[35] Sugden was responsible
for the structural design of the project, which was praised by Simon Bradley for
its 'expressive power' and 'bold articulation'.[36] Barnabas Calder, rightly detect-
ing High-Tech elements in the scheme, comments, 'this is one of Arup Associates' most punchy and exciting buildings'.[37] But Theo Crosby, writing a few
years after the completion of the project, while describing the building as 'cool,
competent, elegant', saw its impact on the city less positively, as 'brutal and
clumsy in its context'. While hesitating to lump it together with recent work by
HKPA, Lasdun and James Stirling, which he described as 'all structural bravura
and vulgar assertion', Crosby felt that its faults were 'part of the modern movement's limitations, of which, after 25 years of intensive construction, we are
now becoming aware'.[38]

A major commercial project, the Lion Yard shopping centre, and new magistrates' courts, commissioned by Cambridge City Council, followed. The practice's association with Cambridge University has continued, with several recent
buildings on the West Cambridge Site. The innovative spirit of Arup Associates
lives on in the Engineering and Computing Building for Coventry University,
completed in 2012 and notable for its low-energy services strategy.

Arup Associates' launch in 1963 came at a time when higher education in
Britain was already expanding rapidly. Alongside the new universities – Sussex
was founded in 1959 – the established 'red brick' and civic institutions were
planning for major growth in student numbers. Oxford and Cambridge, too,
were entering an era of growth and change. Dowson was culturally and socially
in tune with the ethos of Oxbridge. The college projects developed under his
leadership were modern, but equally contextual – even their concrete exoskele-
tons could be criticised as 'soft' modernism by Banham and other leading-edge
critics. As William Whyte has commented, 'in Oxbridge, even high Modernism
was always contextual because architects and their clients shared a fixed set
of beliefs about the nature of the two universities and the cities in which they
had made their home'.[39] So Powell & Moya, HKPA and Arup Associates won
general approval for their Oxbridge projects, while Lasdun and Stirling –
who refused to be contextual – were the subject of widespread opprobrium.

New Museums, Cambridg , 1964–71: interior of the zoological museum

New Museums, Cambridge

The torch of contextual modern design at Oxford and Cambridge was taken up from the 1970s on by Richard MacCormac, Edward Cullinan, Allies and Morrison and others. Context counted for little, however, at Birmingham or Loughborough, and neither university was saddled with the baggage of tradition that a younger generation of Oxbridge academics in the 1950s and 1960s had found so stifling. The Metallurgy and Minerals Building at Birmingham represented another strand in the work of Arup Associates, one rooted in structure and services and in economy of construction. This agenda, driven by Dowson's partners Bob Hobbs and Derek Sugden and taken up energetically by Peter Foggo, was to be central to the development of the practice's work into the 1980s and beyond.

3 Office buildings

The foundation of Ove Arup & Partners in 1946 came as the post-war reconstruction of Britain was just beginning. The urgent need for new housing, schools, factories and hospitals provided ample work for a generation of architects driven, as was Arup himself, by the social ideals of the Modern Movement. While the firm served as structural engineers for many important housing estates and schools, the Building Group founded its success on an ability to produce economical but elegant and structurally innovative factory buildings, largely for new industries. A succession of commissions from IBM for research, production and office buildings confirmed the practice's reputation as a provider of efficient spaces for dynamic businesses, many bridging the divide between office and factory. When Arup Associates was formally established in 1963, Britain's economy was still dominated by manufacturing. Fifty years later, it accounted for only 12 per cent of the nation's GDP and the economy was governed by service industries. The office building became the symbol of economic change.

Arup Associates' earliest office building, completed in 1966, was virtually an in-house commission, an office for Ove Arup & Partners in Edinburgh. The building, modest in size, was sited in the grounds of a Georgian country house. Its structure combined steel beams with precast concrete columns, hollow in form and housing storage shelves. 'The structure becomes a niche and defines and makes a usable space', Michael Brawne commented. 'This very deliberate outlining of a space' became 'very much a preoccupation of its designers and, one suspects, a reaction to the notions of anonymity and an unstated degree of flexibility which has bedevilled so much of present-day architecture'.[1] 'The inhabited space', as Brawne described it, became a defining feature of the Oxbridge college projects, with their agenda of creating 'a sense of belonging' and drove a number of office schemes characterised by a 'spatial definition of almost room-size parts'.[2]

Projects for publishers
Alistair Gourlay, who joined the practice in 1963, had worked on the second building for CIBA at Duxford, and its Miesian simplicity was close to his ideal. In 1966, he began work as project architect for a new complex of offices and warehouse for Penguin Books at Harmondsworth in Middlesex. The site was

Central Electricity Generating Board Regional Headquarters, Bristol, 1973–8 on Bath Road, immediately adjacent to the end of the main Heathrow runway, so one immediate and pressing issue was that of excluding noise and pollution. The use of air conditioning was inevitable. The key feature of the 1370m² building was the heavyweight sandwich roof structure of *in situ* concrete, exposed inside as a coffered ceiling incorporating lighting and air conditioning.

Virtually contemporary with the Penguin project, the new base for the Oxford Mail and Times newspaper group at Osney Mead was typical of many new press buildings of the period, with editorial and management offices linked to a printing plant whose modest size marked a transition from heavy linotype to web offset lithographic printing – a formula that held good before the new technology of the 1980s changed everything. Again, full air conditioning was installed. The offices were single-storey, open-plan, contained within a space 250ft long under

Penguin Books offices and warehouse, Harmondsworth, 1966–72

a precast concrete roof, exposed as a ribbed structure internally and incorporating lighting, heating, ventilation and sprinkler systems. A narrow central spine contained a central corridor with the main services duct above it. The use of yellow brick cladding, exposed internally, gave warmth to the space, fitted out to the architects' specification. Mark Girouard, reviewing the building for the *Architectural Review*, thought the exposed roof structure, externally 'rather over-powering' and a somewhat oppressive feature of the offices. He noted that the project architect, Ulrich Plesner, had previously worked with Geoffrey Bawa in what was then Ceylon, producing what appeared to be hugely enjoyable buildings. 'It has to be admitted', Girouard wrote, 'that the Oxford building does not give the same feeling ... there is a load of Puritanism inherited from the Modern Movement which it is easier to shed in Ceylon than in England'.[3]

Headquarters of the *Oxford Mail* and *Oxford Times*, Osney Mead, Oxford, 1965–71

Lloyd's of London offices, Chatham

The three major bespoke office projects that came to the practice in 1973 reflected a strategy of creating distinct working spaces – with that sense of belonging – defined by structure. They offered a radical alternative to the open-plan office landscapes of North America, which were emulated by British property developers and their architects, and derived some inspiration from Herman Hertzberger's Centraal Beheer at Apeldoorn in the Netherlands, completed in 1972 and widely published in journals. The commissions, from Lloyd's of London, the Central Electricity Generating Board and paper manufacturer Wiggins Teape, came at a time when issues of energy consumption and the environment were much in the air, when the 1973 Yom Kippur War and the resulting oil embargo saw oil prices quadruple. In 1972, RIBA President Alex Gordon declared that 'long life, loose fit, low energy' should be the agenda for the architecture of the future.[4] Gordon's mantra could equally be seen as part of a broader move by the profession to reinvent itself in the face of public revulsion against modernist architecture and planning.

The Lloyd's project originated in a decision by the historic City of London institution to relocate the bulk of its administration out of London. A site reasonably accessible from the capital was required, and the choice fell on Chatham, where there was land along the river Medway, at Gun Wharf close to

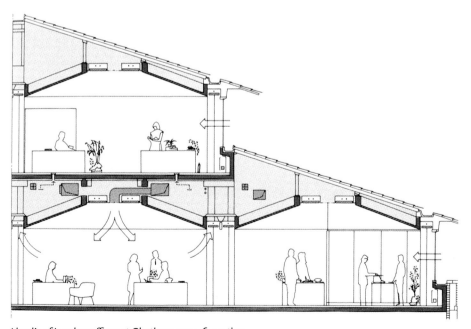

Lloyd's of London offices at Chatham, 1973–6: section

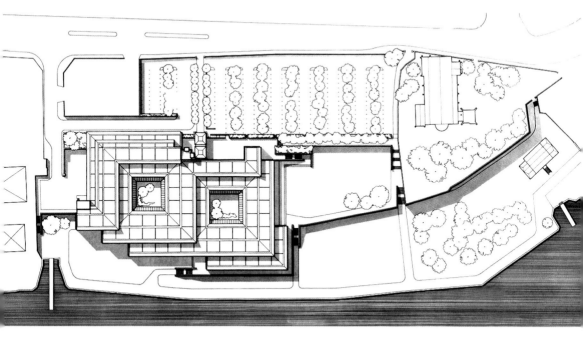

Lloyd's of London offices at Chatham: site plan

the naval dockyard, then still in use by the Royal Navy. This was the site of the original Tudor dockyard. The brief was for a building of around 20,000m², with a very large basement computer room. Lloyd's Head of Administration, Courtenay Blackmore, recalled that 'because of the broadly based, multidisciplinary nature of the firm, Arup Associates were able to ask questions and identify potential problems far more readily than the client'.[5] An open-plan strategy was a fundamental element of the brief.

The initial proposals were for an air-conditioned building, a deep-plan cube that took no account of the contours of the site. Here, however, was an opportunity for the workings of the group system to kick in. As Sam Price (who had moved from Ove Arup & Partners to Arup Associates in 1970) recalled,

> there was a general discussion in the group about fundamentals. The site was large and the air was clean and there were no obvious reasons why a narrow, naturally ventilated building could not be got on to the site. The group generally felt that the architect should reconsider his starting point. I think this view was expressed most forcibly by the structural engineers, who always tended to be the stroppiest.[6]

Lloyd's of London: view across the River Medway

Lloyd's at Chatham, the terrace on the south (land) side of the building

The revised scheme originated in the ideas of the engineers. It provided for a building planned around open courtyards, with relatively narrow office floors, and clusters of four columns, supporting a precast concrete pyramidal ceiling and defining a series of 'tents', each 7.2m × 7.2m in plan, as workspaces. For Blackmore, this approach 'retained the advantages of open plan, but provided a "home" for small groups of staff in each "tent" … In this way the flexibility of open plan combined with a more domestic ambience'.[7]

Clarence McDonald had joined Arup Associates in 1968, working on projects for IBM, but left after three years. Now he was brought back to develop the architectural approach, working with Mike Bonner and Stuart Mercer and engineers Sam Price and Robert Myers, and with Peter Warburton leading on services. Warburton, who joined Group 5 in 1970 to work first on IBM Havant, was a passionate advocate of low-energy design. The offices in the Lloyd's building were naturally ventilated, with air conditioning installed only in the computer suite. The idea of a structural bay defined by a cluster of columns carrying services had been the key feature of the Birmingham University Metallurgy and Minerals Building, completed in 1966, and was adapted with striking

Interior of entrance hall at Lloyd's in Chatham

success to the rather different demands of Lloyd's. The architectural expression of the Chatham building provided a marked contrast to the austere industrial aesthetic of Birmingham. Deliberately contextual, with clear references to the adjacent historic dockyard buildings, the low-rise structure (a maximum of four storeys), with offices around two internal courtyards, was clad in brick, with sloping tiled roofs. It is tempting to read historical references into the architecture – there are certainly echoes of the Prairie houses of Frank Lloyd Wright. The contextual and formal character of the building perhaps facilitated its successful transformation, after Lloyd's vacated it in 2006, into a headquarters for Medway Council. But in essence, this is a building driven by a classic marriage of structure and services.

CEGB Regional Headquarters, Bristol

The commission for a new regional headquarters in Bristol for the Central Electricity Generating Board (CEGB) followed later in 1973. The client brief, developed in consultation with Bob Hobbs as the partner in charge, provided for a building that would replace no fewer than 19 CEGB offices scattered around the Bristol area. The new building, including laboratories and workshops as well as office space, was to be the base for CEGB's activities extending across an area from London to Land's End and Pembrokeshire. Around 1,200 people were to work there. Don Ferguson, the lead architect for the project, had only recently joined Arup Associates after work experience with several practices that included three years in Africa. Ferguson joined Group 5, working on CEGB with Mike Bonner, Nicholas Hare, Mick Brundle and Irving Newman, who had arrived from Skidmore, Owings & Merrill's New York office. Philip Dowson took a close interest in the project: the idea of using pitched roofs appears to have been his.

The site for the new headquarters was – and remains – on the very edge of the city, with an outlook over green fields. The aim was to design a building that would have minimal impact on the landscape and that would be adaptable to changing operational needs. The client wanted a building offering excellent working conditions, with spaces that would give individuals and working groups a sense of identity within the framework of a wider community. Its commitment to that objective was reflected in a commission to the Tavistock Institute for Human Relations to carry out a detailed consultation with staff on what they hoped for in their new workplace. Ferguson remembers CEGB's Peter Vick, who ran the project from the client side, as an exceptional collaborator.

CEGB Regional Headquarters, Bristol: view from the gardens

CEGB Regional Headquarters: detail

The design team explored a number of possible strategies for the site, including the idea of accommodation spread across a series of pavilions to form an academic-style 'campus'. But the final designs created what Tony Marriott (who devised the services strategy for the 24,000m² building) jokingly describes as 'the biggest ranch house in the world':[8] seven connected pavilions around landscaped courtyards, connected by a central 'street'. In common with Lloyd's at Chatham, the CEGB building's architecture has Wrightian undertones. It is 'so well landscaped that offices for 1,200 people facing open countryside all but disappear'.[9] Landscaping was by Peter Swann Associates.

As at Chatham, the environmental and energy agenda was to the fore, as the building was being designed during the 'three-day week'. For Marriott, the project was 'absolutely pioneering – nothing quite like it had been done before'.[10] Overhanging pitched roofs provided solar protection, along with controlled natural light. Clerestory glazing provided daylight to the deeper spaces, minimising the need for artificial lighting. In contrast to Chatham, purely natural ventilation was ruled out in favour of a low-energy mechanical ventilation system. The heavy suspended concrete floor covering the 'industrial' areas below the main office level provided a channel for cool night air to be circulated in summer, offsetting heat gains during the working day. The idea was that cool night air was passed through the interstices of the standard precast floor planks, cooling them down. In winter, a comfortable environment was secured by the use of heat reclaim systems – the laboratories, in particular, generated a lot of heat that was used to warm the swimming pool, a popular staff amenity.

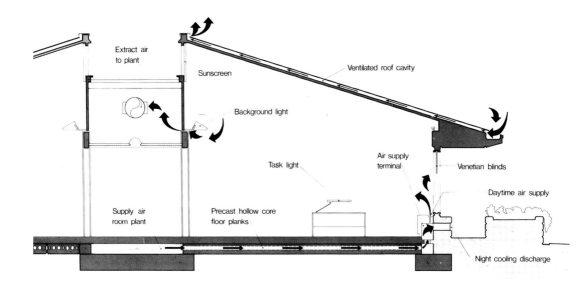

CEGB Regional Headquarters: detailed section showing the ventilation system

Dean Hawkes, in a detailed and not uncritical review of the building's environmental credentials, concluded that 'the building is demonstrably a further step in Arup's thinking. Unlike the cosmetic gestures of some recent office buildings, the nature of this building follows from the interaction between its programme and a way of building'.[11] Here was 'a fertile model for the design of office buildings'.[12] Richard MacCormac, reviewing the project in the *Architectural Review* contrasted it with the classic modernist formula for offices 'in which the physical presence of architecture itself, structure and form, and their corresponding potential for enclosure, have been further suppressed and dissolved to achieve a neutrality of space in which people and furniture can be most flexibly disposed'. Avoiding the extreme multicellular approach of Hertzberger, Arup Associates had made 'an important contribution to the middle ground of this polemic', in many respects creating a more comprehensible and less repetitive building than the Centraal Beheer.[13] The demise of the CEGB left the building redundant, but, rebranded The Pavilions, it is now occupied by a leading data company.

Gateway Houses 1 and 2, Basingstoke

The third major office project launched in 1973 adopted an architectural language that contrasted with the Wrightian contextualism of Lloyd's and CEGB – though there were close parallels in its organisational strategy. The client for Gateway House 1 at Basingstoke was Wiggins Teape, a company with a history in paper manufacture extending back to the 18th century, which was relocating its offices, and 1,000 staff, from Central London. The project was undertaken by Peter Foggo's Group 2.

If the aesthetic of the building appeared strongly North American, its planning was in a European tradition. Foggo's admiration for the work of Mies emerged strongly at Gateway 1, with its tinted glazing and bronze anodized metal cladding supplied by Gartners of Munich, but the influence of Hertzberger's recently completed Centraal Beheer is equally apparent. Foggo had taken his team to visit Apeldoorn, and the Centraal Beheer's stepped roof terraces influenced the Basingstoke project. The tartan grid plan adopted by Hertzberger had been prefigured in Arup Associates' Birmingham laboratory building a decade earlier, and the idea of a repeated ceiling bay, with structure and services integrated into a human-scaled workspace, was a feature of the CEGB and Lloyd's projects. Offices were accommodated on five floors, with a large basement for car parking. The most striking feature of Gateway 1 is the series of planted roof gardens extending over the stepped southern elevation, designed by the landscape architect James Russell and Charles Funke, and providing a remarkable amenity for staff working there. The building, which was listed in 2015, is now known as Mountbatten House.

Overleaf: Gateway House 1, Basingstoke, for Wiggins Teape, 1973–6

Gateway 1, Basingstoke: interior of restaurant, showing characteristic coffered ceilings

Gateway House 1 was completed in 1976, but within a few years, Wiggins Teape decided, in the light of a reduction in the number of staff employed there, to sell the building – at a considerable profit – and to move into Gateway House 2, a building on an adjacent site by Arup Associates that had been designed initially for letting. The brief for Gateway 2 was to design a building for fast-track delivery, to complement Gateway 1 and with the potential to be let.

Completed in 1982, Gateway 2 was another exercise in low-energy design. Externally, the building had a family resemblance to Gateway 1, but its internal diagram was radically different, focusing on a full-height central atrium. The atrium was conceived as the hub of the building, in social and circulation terms – it housed badminton matches after office hours – but was equally the key to a system of natural ventilation, with opening roof vents channelling fresh air into the office areas. In winter, the atrium was warmed using reclaimed heat from the building's computer suite. Exposing the concrete structure in the office floors provided a thermal mass to reduce extremes of temperature. The atrium itself was a virtuoso exercise in steelwork design, prefiguring the use of steel as the basic structural material at Finsbury Avenue and Broadgate. Using a management contract, the project was completed to budget and to an 18-month construction schedule. In due course, as a result of Wiggins Teape's merger into an international manufacturing combine, Gateway 2 was vacated and sold off. The new owners chose to re-equip the building with air conditioning, a change at odds with the intentions of its designers but one it was able to seamlessly accommodate.

Gateway 2, Basingstoke, 1981–2: interior of atrium as completed

Developments in the City

Gateway House 2 (now known as Belvedere House) was to be a landmark project for the practice, not least for its successful use of fast-track construction strategies. Arup Associates' office projects to date, including the very large headquarters building for IBM at Cosham, constructed in several phases, the last completed in 1982, had been bespoke – tailored to the specific needs of prestige clients. Gateway 2 was conceived as a lettable building, essentially a speculative development. The 1960s boom in speculative office development in London had generated a great deal of work for architects, but Arup Associates, like other critically acclaimed practices, declined to become involved. As late as the early 1980s, when Peter Foggo's team took on Finsbury Avenue and Broadgate, there were those in the office who felt that working for developers was somehow undignified. But in 1971, the practice accepted a commission from developer Trafalgar House for an office development, Bush Lane House, adjacent to Cannon Street station in the City of London. There was one issue that had to be addressed immediately. The site (just 1027m² in extent) lay directly above that of a proposed new Underground station, part of the Fleet Line, the precursor of the Jubilee Line (which was rerouted, in the event, beyond the City).

The office development had to provide for the construction of the station box, so that piles for the building had to avoid the proposed subterranean tunnels and passageways. At ground level, it had to provide a 10m-high space for the station ticket hall. The design strategy drew fully on the multidisciplinary skills of the office. American-born Dick Raines (1929–2016, formerly with Architects' Co-Partnership, where he had been project architect for Dunelm House at Durham University) was project architect, working with John Brandenburger and structural engineer Michael Eatherley. Foundations were concentrated into four pairs of circular columns supporting an external lattice-steel frame that sidestepped the proposed tube line and left internal spaces free of structural divisions. The external frame of the eight-storey building consisted of a lattice of welded stainless-steel tubes on a diagonal grid, forming a delicate screen set forward and independent of the glazed curtain wall. An exposed steel frame was at odds with London building regulations, but the steel tubes were filled with water so as to make the frame fire resistant. This was the strategy being applied contemporaneously at the Centre Georges Pompidou in Paris, where Ove Arup & Partners, under Ted Happold and Peter Rice, were working with the architects Piano & Rogers. The technical formula for the water-filled frame having been developed, the issue of how it was to be fabricated arose. Structural steelwork contractors had no experience of using stainless steel in this way and the precision casting of the steel members was eventually carried out by APV Paramount, a company that manufactured equipment for the dairy and brewing industries. It was a classic instance of the 'technology transfer' that became a feature of the High-Tech school of design emerging in the 1970s.

Bush Lane House, Cannon Street, London, 1970–6

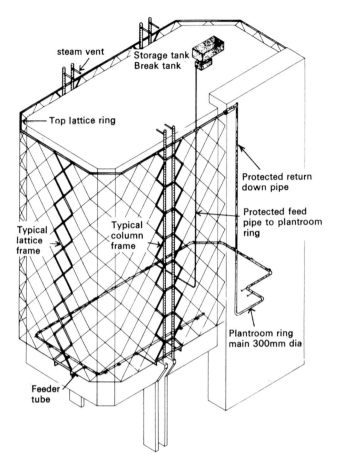

steam vent

Storage tank
Break tank

Top lattice ring

Protected return
down pipe

Protected feed
pipe to plantroom
ring

Typical
lattice
frame

Typical
column
frame

Plantroom ring
main 300mm dia

Feeder
tube

Bush Lane House: diagram showing design for water-filled external frame

During the 1980s, the economic climate of Britain changed. Margaret Thatcher's Conservative government, elected in 1979, was content to allow the further decline of the country's manufacturing sector, while privatisation saw bodies such as the CEGB extinguished. Yet financial services boomed. A key landmark in the emergence of the new economy was the so-called 'Big Bang' of 1986, which saw the London stock market, previously a closed shop and widely viewed as an old boys' club, opened up to global competition. International investment banks, many of them American, opened offices in London. Trading in stocks and shares, previously conducted on the floor of the Stock Exchange by brokers and jobbers, was henceforth to be conducted by telephone or on computer screens. New buildings were needed to accommodate traders on large dealing floors and the question arose whether the City, the historic heart of the financial services industry, could accommodate such buildings?

The solution, it was argued, was to relocate the big banks to virgin territory in London Docklands, an 'enterprise zone' where planning controls had been virtually abolished as part of a campaign to revitalise an area left desolate by the decline of the Port of London. The result was the rise of Canary Wharf as a new business district, developed with high-rise buildings to a master plan by the American practice Skidmore Owings & Merrill.

Nos. 1–3 Finsbury Avenue, London

A key element in the City's successful fight-back against Docklands was Broadgate, developed on former railway land on its fringes close to Liverpool Street station. The developer was Rosehaugh Stanhope, an alliance between financier Godfrey Bradman and developer Stuart Lipton. As a partner in Greycoat Properties, Lipton had completed a major office development at Cutlers' Gardens on the eastern edge of the City in 1982. A mix of reconstructed 18th-century warehouses and new build, the development was designed by Richard Seifert & Partners, a practice in the forefront of the commercial development scene since the early 1960s. Lipton's decision to commission Arup Associates to design the entire first phase of Broadgate was a landmark move. But before Broadgate there was Finsbury Avenue.

1–3 Finsbury Avenue, London, 1981–4

1 Finsbury Avenue: detail of façade

Lipton had been introduced to the work of Arup Associates by his old friend Jack Zunz of Ove Arup & Partners. He had seen the CEGB, Lloyd's and Gateway projects – he was especially impressed by Gateway 2 – and decided to approach the practice in 1981, when the opportunity arose to develop offices on part of the Broad Street station site just west of Liverpool Street. The site, a former goods yard that had been turned over to car parking some years before, was actually just within the London Borough of Hackney – though boundary changes in the 1990s brought it into the City. The design team from Group 2 included Peter Foggo, Bruce Vickers, Tony Taylor, Ian Taylor and Peter Skead.

The aim was to get a highly efficient building completed to a fast-track schedule. Foggo's first scheme for the site proposed an exposed concrete structure, but Lipton was insistent on the use of a steel-framed structure with metal deck floor slabs on the North American model.

The break with Foggo's earlier projects was radical, and not one he found easy to accept. But eventually he agreed that the client's formula had to be adopted. Foggo and team travelled to the USA to study current American practice. They were dismayed by the quality of construction on some of the projects they saw and concerned about the implications for architects in a system where construction managers were becoming dominant. Nonetheless, the concept for No. 1 Finsbury Avenue was developed rapidly by Foggo – Lipton recalled Sunday morning meetings in Arup Associates' offices, at that time located in Soho Square. The building was to be completed to 'shell and core', ready for tenants to fit out. Foggo wrote that 'the design must recognise the difference between those parts of the building with a long, stable life span and those where constant change, wide variation in aesthetic character and short life are principal characteristics'.[14] Foggo was equally clear, having seen American construction strategies at first hand, that an uncritical adoption of them would be a mistake. 'It can lead to the de-architecturalisation of architecture. The emphasis is on repetitive simplicity rather than ingenuity as a way of achieving cheapness. It can turn architects into shoppers rather than designers.'[15]

Skead developed the structural diagram for No. 1 Finsbury Avenue, based on a 6m grid. The 25,000m² building went on site late in 1982 and was completed in September 1984 using a management contract strategy with Laings as pioneered by Foggo at the Horizon Factory in Nottingham. Internally, the building was focused on a full-height central atrium, later partly infilled, which recalled that at Gateway House 2, though No. 1 Finsbury Avenue was air conditioned throughout. Externally, it was clad in a bronze anodized cladding system, again developed by the German manufacturer Gartner, incorporating a perimeter heating system. Setbacks, sun-shading and strongly expressed stair towers helped to break down the mass of the building. Indeed, it was the external aspect of the building that impressed critics, who were less interested in its radical commercial agenda.

The *Architectural Review* commented that 'Arups have provided an object lesson for all architects. They prove that spec offices can make a sensitive contribution to a civic environment, and that even a huge office building can have a richness and delicate scale suggestive of the human beings who work within'.[16] In commercial terms, the development had been something of a gamble, but it was quickly completely let. The first tenants were mostly lawyers, and the big floors were subdivided, some with neo-Georgian panelling, but the entire building was later taken over by a big bank. In 1997, an Arup Associates team led by Mick Brundle was responsible for major internal alterations, including the flooring over of the atrium to create large dealing-floor spaces. These changes notwithstanding, No. 1 Finsbury Avenue was listed in 2015.

1 Finsbury Avenue: atrium before subdivision

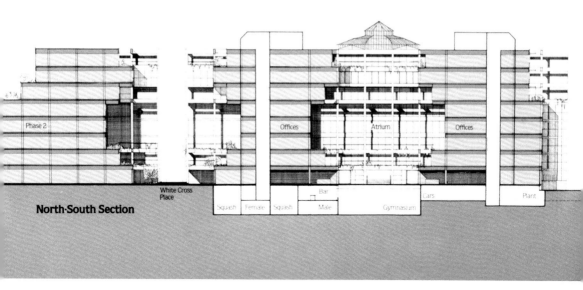

1 Finsbury Avenue: section

Foggo's original concept had always provided for further phases of development on Wilson and Sun streets, potentially forming part of a new square, and Nos. 2 and 3 Finsbury Avenue were subsequently constructed in 1985–8, their architectural vocabulary very much in the mould of No. 1, and both built to a management contract administered by Laings. No. 3 Finsbury Avenue, the smallest of the three at 10,000m², featured a double-skin glazed façade, a device already employed by the practice at Briarcliff House, an office development in Farnborough completed in 1983.

The Broadgate development

When No. 1 Finsbury Avenue was completed, Broad Street station was still open. Demolition did not begin until late in 1985, following the failure of conservationist attempts to have the frontage preserved, and the last train ran (from a single working platform) in June 1986. In 1985, British Rail signed an agreement with Lipton and Bradman to redevelop the remainder of the station site. In the same year, BR began a redevelopment of Liverpool Street station, retaining the listed western train shed and Great Eastern Hotel and demolishing the eastern half of the station, providing a site for the later phases of Broadgate. Even as 1 Finsbury Avenue was being completed in 1984, Foggo was working on the plans for Broadgate, liaising with BR's architect, Nick Derbyshire, to ensure that the layout dovetailed with that for Liverpool Street. Stuart Lipton recalled that 'typically for him, it had no designs for buildings, but an analysis of spaces'.[17]

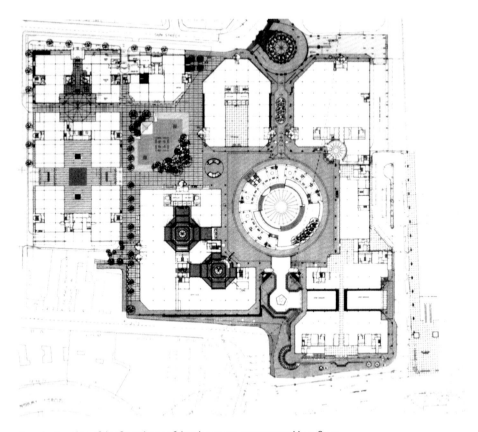

Broadgate: plan of the first phase of development, constructed in 1985–7

Fast-track construction to shell and core was fundamental to Broadgate. The Arup team, including again Peter Skead and Tony Taylor in an expanded group numbering around 25, further developed the strategy applied at Finsbury Avenue for the first phases of development, with work on site beginning in 1985. Phases 1–4, completed in 1987, consisted of four blocks around a central square (now Broadgate Circle), all constructed on a steel frame with concrete slab floors on steel decking. An open atrium was a feature of all the buildings, each distinct in form though none as impressive as that at No. 1 Finsbury Avenue. Cladding was brought to site as pre-assembled bay-width units, and toilet units were prefabricated off-site (as they had been at Richard Rogers's newly completed Lloyd's Building). In contrast to the metallic cladding of Finsbury Avenue, polished granite was used, in the form of perforated brise-soleil screens set forward of the main façades, since, as Stuart Lipton recalls, 'Peter Rees [then the City's chief planner] was determined to have masonry facades'.[18] Foggo's use of stone made clear that it was a nonstructural device, though one would hesitate to use the word decorative.

Broadgate Arena, before recent alterations

The architecture of the Broadgate buildings, blander than that of No. 1 Finsbury Avenue, has been rather less admired than the public spaces in which they sit.[19] Rab Bennetts, who joined the practice direct from college in 1977 and stayed 10 years before establishing Bennetts Associates, spending eight years in Group 2, thought that Broadgate was 'too fast for its own good ... The buildings suffered a great deal from the lack of design time'.[20] The circular road at basement level connecting all the buildings allowed Broadgate to become a totally traffic-free environment. The commercial success of the buildings was assured: in the excitement of the Big Bang of 1986, they were quickly let to financial institutions and easily accommodated new-style dealing floors. What generated enthusiastic comment at the time of their completion was the procurement and constructional process that underpinned the project, built to a management contract, run by Bovis under project director Ian Macpherson, which pioneered in Britain the American strategy of 'value engineering'. (The American construction management firm Schal had an important advisory role in the project.) Broadgate was acclaimed as being 'very much in the forefront of technological innovation in this country. Chances are that, in a few years' time, UK construction will be divided into two eras – pre and post-Broadgate'.[21] Designed for a lifespan of half a century, the Arup buildings at Broadgate are being steadily replaced as part of an ongoing strategy of renewal for the estate. Two blocks on the north side of the central public space, Broadgate Circle, have been replaced by the 5 Broadgate development, designed by Make Architects, and others are set to follow.

Broadgate: Buildings 4 and 6, now demolished

The Stockley Park project

Lipton effectively reinvented the City office building at Broadgate. Equally significant was his role in pioneering the out-of-town business park, for which Stockley Park, close to the M4 motorway and Heathrow Airport, provided the template. The initial idea of developing the 140ha site, largely occupied by a vast rubbish dump, came from a relatively small company, Trust Securities, which was unable to fund the project. In 1983, Lipton, in partnership with Elliott Bernerd, stepped in to progress it. Again, Lipton turned to Arup Associates. With Foggo's Group 2 working on Finsbury Avenue and Broadgate, Dowson turned to Michael Lowe (South African born, and a member of what was jokingly described as the Arup 'Safia') and his colleagues in Group 6 to develop a scheme for economical two- and three-storey buildings set in an attractive landscape. The Arup master plan was developed to a brief prepared by John Worthington of DEGW. This provided for a development allowing the centralisation under one roof of research and design, product assembly and customisation, and market and consumer services.

When the Stockley project was launched, the site was still zoned for industrial use, but under the Thatcher reforms, a new use category (B1), covering office, research and light manufacturing, was introduced, and opened the way for the further development of the Stockley concept. With the site cleared, including the shifting of a huge quantity of waste 9m deep, construction work began in 1985. By 1987, eight buildings by Arup Associates had been completed: steel-framed two-storey pavilions with 18m-deep floors and central atria. Architecturally straightforward, with hipped roofs and white cladding, they injected an overall discipline into Stockley, though a number of other practices were subsequently brought in to design buildings there in more expressive modes.

Michael Lowe concedes that 'the landscape was the key to the project – Stuart was absolutely committed to creating something excellent. We looked at some of the great French gardens as exemplars, working with the garden designer Charles Funke'.[22] A series of lakes and canals was a key feature. Arup Associates, under architects David Thomas, Peter Foggo and Richard Frewer, with Terry Raggett and Charles Wymer as engineers, were responsible for further phases of Stockley – including the Arena, intended to be the social heart of the development and opened in 1989. Following the hiatus in development during the recession of the 1990s, the practice returned again, this time under James Burland, for the buildings comprising The Square (1996–8). The diagram of the early Arup blocks at Stockley was now inverted to provide cruciform floorplates around a central service core, enclosed within a glazed outer façade that provided a buffer zone of atrium space with the potential for naturally ventilating the buildings.[23]

Overleaf: Stockley Park, Hayes, 1985–7: standard units in Roundwood Avenue, from across the lake

The Arena shops and services building, Stockley Park, 1988–9

Arup Associates' spectacular entry into the field of speculative office design was by no means uncontroversial within the practice, with Dowson, in particular, having qualms about this new departure. But the development world was changing, after Lipton had declared that 'good architecture pays'. Soon, Norman Foster, Richard Rogers and others were also designing spec office buildings. Foggo's Group 2 had generated a large amount of fee income for Arup Associates. Bennetts admired 'the cohesive nature of the group and its loyalty to Peter ... His formidable powers of persuasion ensured that the strategic direction of any scheme was never in doubt'. Bennetts recalled that 'clients were generally captivated by Peter's personality, combined with the coherence of the team and its ability to produce building after building on time and on budget'. He also admired the fact that 'Peter Foggo led by example. He had a knack of empowering members of the team whilst remaining in undisputed control ... He didn't have a monopoly on ideas, but was usually the most radical thinker in the group, not only in design terms but also on issues such as contract innovations, relationships with contractors and construction techniques'.[24] In 1989, Foggo left Arup Associates, taking a number of Group 2 members with him, and successfully established his own office. He died four years later, aged only 62.

No. 4 The Square, Stockley Park, 1995–8: the centrepiece of the last phase

Interior of The Arena at Stockley Park

Bespoke buildings for company headquarters

Speculative offices remained an important part of the practice's workload
after Foggo's departure, but the demand for one-off bespoke headquarters
buildings also stayed strong. Insurance companies were to the fore. Legal
& General's new headquarters at Kingswood, Surrey, a relocation from
central London, was completed in 1988 by a team led by Don Ferguson as
architect, Terry Raggett as structural engineer, and with Peter Warburton
again in charge of services design. This project further developed the low-
energy strategy pioneered at Lloyd's of Chatham and CEGB, Bristol, with a
heat storage system using the swimming pool (provided as one of a number of
exceptional staff amenities) as a heat sink. Extensive shading baffled solar gain.

Legal and General headquarters, Banstead, 1986–91: entrance

Ferguson recalls the project as 'difficult in political terms' – there were local objections to development in the Green Belt, though Legal & General had occupied buildings on the site since the 1940s. The three-storey building was designed on a rigorously symmetrical plan around two landscaped courtyards. The concrete columns carrying the external sun-screening gave the building a mildly classical look, but this theme was more fully developed in the impressive rotunda that formed the entrance to the complex. This was inspired by John Soane and Edwin Lutyens, and some in the practice felt that it was a step too far in the direction of post-modernism. The Legal & General headquarters was set in an impressive landscape incorporating sports pitches and tennis courts.

Legal and General headquarters, Banstead: interior

The landscape theme was further developed by Alistair Gourlay and his team in new offices at Peterborough for Royal Life, completed in 1991. The building was designed to embrace views to the open countryside, extending down to the river Nene, to the north of the site. A 180m-long, 12m-high glazed screen wall set forward of the concrete-framed office floors formed the defining feature of the northern elevation, which was prefaced by formal gardens. A staff restaurant, sports hall and other communal spaces were located in a curved southern block, steel framed and separated from the offices by an internal 'street' with a solid roof to ensure a temperate internal climate. Offices were serviced by a low-energy ventilation system. The landscape theme extended to the car park on the south (entrance) side of the building, where the restaurant spilled out on to a terrace overlooking a sizeable lake.[25]

Offices for Royal Life (now Lynchwood House), Peterborough, 1987–91

Royal Life offices: interior

Royal Life offices: screen wall to north elevation

The last and largest of a series of what seem, in retrospect, quite lavish bespoke headquarters projects was that for the retail division of Lloyds Bank, completed in 1991 on a waterfront site at Canon's Marsh, Bristol. The site, formerly occupied by bonded warehouses and owned by the City Council, had been identified as critical to the regeneration of the city's docklands, but the local authority was reluctant to see it developed for offices. It took pressure from Whitehall, Don Ferguson admits, to progress the scheme. The paired precast concrete columns along the curved, symmetrical crescent forming the elevation to the Floating Harbour gave the building a strongly classical flavour – again, post-modernist tendencies were detected. There were some parallels with Arup Associates' unbuilt Paternoster Square scheme.

Lloyds headquarters, Canon's Marsh, Bristol, 1988–91

Ferguson, who led the design team, assisted by Stuart Mercer, recalls tensions between the client (looking for a 'safe' design) and the planners, who wanted something more innovative. A second phase of development took the form of a circular 'doughnut' to the rear, its elevation again using the language of columns on a solid base. The innovative elements of the scheme were found in its services strategy, using natural convection to supplement the ventilation system and dock water for cooling. The building was popular with the public, but was widely seen as architecturally compromised. 'The design shuns the carefully cultured 1980s dockside aesthetic in favour of Beaux-Arts planning and civic gestures', was the comment in The Buildings of England series guide, while Tony Aldous found it inappropriate to the location and wasteful of space, albeit admitting that the scheme was a catalyst to the revival of Bristol's waterfront.[26]

Lloyds, Canon's Marsh, Bristol: interior

Office buildings for a new century

The decisive move into speculative office development led by Foggo established Arup Associates as a major player in the field. Mick Brundle, who joined the practice in 1975, was lead architect, succeeding David Thomas, for the 100,000m² Plantation Place development in the City of London, completed in 2004 with British Land as client. The scheme was built on the site of Plantation House, a massive 1930s complex that had been comprehensively refurbished in the early 1990s. The project had started badly, when a proposal for a spiralling tower had met with outright opposition from the City. The maximum height for a building on the site was now established as 70m on Fenchurch Street, stepping down to the south where the setting of Wren's church of St Margaret Pattens was a major issue. The brief was effectively for a 'banking factory' with very large floor plates.

Plantation Place, City of London, 1996–2006

The built scheme provided for two buildings, a block stepping up to 15 storeys on Fenchurch Street and a 10-storey block on Eastcheap/Great Tower Street. The northern block was extensively glazed, but the lower floors were equipped with stone fins, a response to the planners' taste for solidity but recalling the layered façades of Arup Associates' Oxbridge college buildings of the 1960s and 1970s. The upper floors were clad in a double-skin façade that allowed for mixed-mode ventilation, with natural cross ventilation on top floors.

Section through Plantation Place

The southern block was given a load-bearing stone façade with more limited glazing. Between the two buildings, a new east–west pedestrian route, Plantation Lane, was created – a real public gain. The interior featured one of the most impressive atria in the City.

Idealism was not necessarily a dominant theme in the cut-throat development world of the early 21st century, but the concern for making workplaces offering something beyond the purely functional – with thought given to the users of buildings – was a theme that looked back to the early years of Arup Associates and the humanistic philosophy of Ove Arup, who wanted 'the warm humanity of art to permeate the cold economics of efficient building'.[27]

4 Public buildings and conversions

When Arup Associates was launched in 1963, the Modern Movement reigned triumphant over the British architectural scene. A decade later, the mood had changed – and the practice's architecture responded to that shift. Projects such as those for Lloyd's of London in Chatham and CEGB in Bristol reflected the move towards contextual design and a concern for sustainability.[1] Arup Associates' potent technical expertise in the area of services engineering gave it a lead in the development of low-energy design, for which the oil crisis of 1973 provided a powerful catalyst. The 1970s was also a decade in which the forces of community and conservation impacted strongly on the work of the architectural profession.

The conversion of old buildings was not a major concern of the generation of architects, including Philip Dowson, who came to prominence in the post-war years. But working with historic buildings came to be an important element in the workload of Arup Associates.

The Snape Maltings Concert Hall

A landmark project was the conversion of part of the complex of maltings at Snape in Suffolk to house a concert hall, which became the principal base of the Aldeburgh Festival. East Anglia had resonances for some of the leading figures in Arup Associates. Dowson's family home was in Norfolk and he was responsible for two private houses in Suffolk, at Monks Eleigh, completed in 1959, and at Acton near Long Melford, completed in 1964, the latter designed with extensive input from Peter Foggo and David Thomas.[2]

Derek Sugden had begun attending the Aldeburgh Festival, founded on a modest scale by Benjamin Britten in 1948, in 1957, and he often holidayed on the Suffolk coast. Music was Sugden's great passion, inherited, he suggested, from his mother, a fine amateur singer. As a teenager, he had attended Proms at the Queen's Hall in London, before it was destroyed by bombs in 1941. So when Ove Arup asked him to go to Aldeburgh and discuss with Britten the possible creation of a new, permanent home for the Festival, Sugden eagerly embarked on what became the most significant project of his long career.

H T ('Jim') Cadbury-Brown had produced several abortive proposals for an opera house in Aldeburgh, where Festival concerts took place in the less than perfect setting of the Jubilee Hall. In 1965, Britten decided that the redundant maltings at Snape (where he had lived for a time) could provide the home that

Snape Maltings, 1965–7: interior

Williams House (Long Wall), Long Melford, 1962–4: exterior by night

Williams House (Long Wall): the main internal space

the expanding Festival so badly needed. Sugden met first Stephen Reiss and then Britten, with his partner, Peter Pears. Britten was from the start a demanding client. The raw material for the new hall, 'a concert hall with certain facilities for opera', was the New House, a huge industrial space filled with drying kilns, long disused and in very poor condition. Britten, Sugden recalled, had no clear idea of how much the conversion would cost or how the money would be raised – simply total confidence that the project would succeed. 'Britten wanted up to 1,000 seats and told me that the cost should be no more than £50,000. And the hall should be open for the 1966 Festival!'[3]

The final cost of the project was £127,000: Britten agreed that completion of the hall (seating 830) in time for the 1967 Festival was a practical objective. The Arup team, which included architects John Brandenburger and Colin Dollimore and the engineer Max Fordham, set out to combine the new facilities required while retaining the industrial character of the maltings. Work started on site in

Peter Pears, Derek Sugden and Benjamin Britten
in the ruins of the gutted Snape Maltings

Snape Maltings: interior, looking from stage

March 1966. Sugden later wrote that 'the roof design was the key to the whole building'.[4] A central dividing wall had to be removed and the height of the interior raised to provide the volume required to give a sufficient reverberation time for music. The maltings' characteristic rooftop smoke hoods were a feature Sugden felt should be retained and these were reconstructed on the rebuilt roof. The stage spanned the whole width of the hall, with raked seating allowing plant and toilets to be located below the auditorium. Dressing rooms and other facilities were located in a two-storey building conveniently placed to the rear, overlooking the marshes around the Alde estuary. The roof of untreated timber, brick walls simply grit blasted and left much as found, hardwood floors and pine doors were part of the industrial aesthetic of the hall and further aided the acoustic. The cane timber seating was modelled on that in Wagner's Festspielhaus at Bayreuth after Imogen Holst, Britten's assistant, argued that the seats 'mustn't be too comfortable … They should make people sit properly'.[5]

Snape Maltings: exterior, with top-floor restaurant added to designs by Penoyre & Prasad in 1999

Acoustics was a key issue: Britten, like many musicians, particularly disliked that of the Royal Festival Hall. Sugden was sceptical about the 'pseudo-scientific' approach to acoustic design, and believed that two of the churches near Aldeburgh used for Festival concerts, Orford and Blythburgh, had near perfect acoustics. His pragmatic approach was founded on the belief that it was 'dangerous to talk about acoustics in an abstract way, to divorce them from their physical surroundings, because the whole architecture of the space in which music is made is as much responsible for our whole response to the music'.[6] In the event, the acoustics of the hall, devised by Sugden with the assistance of Fordham, proved to be perfect even to Britten's ears. Music critics pronounced it one of the best in Britain, a reputation it retains to this day.

The Snape Maltings Concert Hall was officially opened by HM The Queen in June, 1967. Two years later, on 7 June 1969, following the first evening of the Festival, it was gutted by fire. Sugden got a telephone call at 7 o'clock the next morning, a Sunday, and was soon on his way to the site, where he met Britten and Pears gloomily surveying the smoking shell. Britten told a tearful Sugden that he and Pears had come to terms with the tragedy and that the hall had to be rebuilt right away 'just as it was'. A team had to be assembled rapidly.

A key person was site foreman Bill Muttitt from Blythburgh, whom Britten insisted on being recalled from another building project. 'Ove thought Bill was exceptional', Sugden recalled. 'Why can't we have people like him on all our jobs, he asked'.[7] The rebuilding was completed in 42 weeks, in time for the 1970 Festival. John Braithwaite, who had recently joined the practice, was the site architect – his love of music had helped when he was interviewed by Sugden, and Snape was the first of a number of musical projects on which they worked together.

Other musical and theatrical projects

The Music School at the new University of East Anglia was completed in 1973, contextual in its own way in deferring to the architecture of Denys Lasdun's campus. Two further projects came to the practice in 1972. The London Symphony and London Philharmonic orchestras had come together to develop a new rehearsal space in London. There was the idea of converting a disused church and the choice eventually fell on the neo-classical Regency church of Holy Trinity, Southwark, which had been closed in 1960 and was nearly derelict. But before work on conversion could begin, it was gutted by fire. The conversion scheme that had already been drawn up provided for a very tactful approach to the new use, respecting the character of the building, internally and externally. The fire might have prompted a more radical approach, but Sugden and his team stuck with their original proposals for the Henry Wood Hall, as the converted building was named, and the interior was carefully reconstructed, with the destroyed western gallery reinstated. The crypt, where large numbers of corpses had to be removed, was converted into a cafeteria for the musicians, with the floor lowered.

Fire also figured in the history of the second project initiated in 1972. The Theatre Royal, Glasgow, a late Victorian theatre by C J Phipps, had been used as television studios before its acquisition by Scottish Opera with the aim of making it an opera house for Scotland. In 1970, however, it was badly damaged by fire. Working to a very tight budget, the Arup team, with Braithwaite and Richard Frewer as architects working alongside Sugden, rebuilt the auditorium in an authentic manner. The new foyer was done in matching style – there were no qualms about 'pastiche' and the marriage of old and new is seamless, though The Buildings of Scotland editors thought the foyer spaces 'surprisingly cramped' and regretted the toning down of the original colour scheme in the auditorium.[8]

An equally tactful approach informed the restoration of the Opera House at Buxton, Derbyshire, completed in 1979. On the basis of these commissions, Sugden, in partnership with Richard Cowell who had been a consultant for the Snape project, launched Arup Acoustics in 1980. Sugden remained a partner in Arup Associates, chairing the practice in 1983–7, while acting as a consultant on projects such as the Glyndebourne Opera House and Bridgewater Hall, Manchester.

Henry Wood Hall, Southwark, 1979–81: the main interior

Other public building conversions

'The most intricate interweaving of old and new which the practice has carried out' was Michael Brawne's comment on the offices for Babergh District Council at Hadleigh in Suffolk, completed in 1982.[9] The project, in which Philip Dowson took a close interest, combined new build with the careful conversion of former farm buildings. Richard Frewer, who worked on it, was also lead architect for the new additions to Ampleforth College in Yorkshire, a public school run by the monks of Ampleforth Abbey, where Basil Hume was then Abbot. A derelict and undistinguished late Georgian building was demolished for a new development providing new teaching and residential space. Part of the challenge posed by the project was establishing a line of communication between the new buildings and the disparate collection of structures already on the site, which were mostly Victorian Gothic in style but were dominated by the abbey church designed by Giles Gilbert Scott. Again, the designs were contextual in manner, with a touch,

Babergh District Council Offices, Hadleigh, 1977–82

at least, of Frank Lloyd Wright, and the concrete blockwork forming the raw material of the new additions was toned in with the stone of the older buildings.

One of Arup Associates' least-known projects of the early 1980s, the reconstruction after a destructive fire in 1979 of part of Bedford School, displayed a virtuosic skill in the use of timber. The school's gutted Great Hall was rebuilt with a magnificent new roof, featuring interlocking timber vaults braced by a boarded ceiling of cedar. Julian Bicknell, a recent recruit to the practice who had previously worked with Edward Cullinan, acted as project architect under Dowson before setting up his own practice and establishing a reputation as a 'new classicist'. In fact, working in timber, rather than steel and concrete, was not entirely at odds with the ethos of Arup Associates. Wooden models, made in the practice's famously talented model shop, were an essential tool in the development of any project and it is tempting to see Dowson's approach to the use of precast concrete as an adaptation of a language of timber construction.

The Great Hall, Bedford School

The Imperial War Museum came to Arup Associates in 1983 with a brief to draw up a strategy for its future development, increasing gallery space and providing enhanced visitor facilities within its existing 19th-century building, which had begun as the Bethlem Royal Hospital and had housed the museum since 1936. The first phases of development in 1986–9 provided a spectacular addition, a galleried central hall with an overall translucent glazed roof in what had been an open court-yard. This afforded an ideal space for the display of historic aircraft, tanks and other military hardware. New galleries for the museum's art collection and a cinema were also created. The second phase of the development infilled a lightwell in the south-eastern corner of the building to create more gallery spaces. Finally, a third phase, completed in 2000, gave the museum more display space, conference and education facilities and accommodation for the Holocaust Museum.[10] Arup Associates' work at the museum has now been obscured – and some would say compromised – by the major project there by Foster + Partners, completed in 2014.

New Central Hall, Imperial War Museum, London, 1986–2000

5 Later works

Ove Arup died in 1988, and the younger founding fathers of the firm departed around the same time. The retirement of Philip Dowson in 1990, following the resignation of Derek Sugden as Chairman the previous year, was inevitably something of a watershed for Arup Associates. Dowson had been knighted in 1980, and in 1981 received the Royal Gold Medal for Architecture – although some felt that it should have gone to the practice collectively. In 1993, he became President of the Royal Academy of Arts. Peter Foggo had quit in 1989 to set up his own practice, taking much of his talented Group 2 team with him. His last project for Arup Associates, completed in 1990, was the office and retail development at No. 123 Buckingham Palace Road, an air-rights scheme straddling the rail tracks into London's Victoria Station and set behind a retained Victorian screen wall. Structurally ingenious and making use of Group 2's experience with steel-framed construction, the project was architecturally rather matter of fact, its exposed steelwork recalling some giant Meccano set.

In the 1990s Arup Associates, in common with other practices, faced the challenge of a recession, which saw new commissions dry up and projects put on hold or cancelled. Staff had to be laid off, and the group system, which had been so fundamental to the practice from its foundation, appeared to be breaking down. Arup Associates was still seen as a front-rank British practice, but it could not avoid the fall-out from the 'style wars' of the 1980s, fuelled by HRH The Prince of Wales, whose comments had led to the cancellation of its Paternoster Square project (*see* pp 114–16). In a pluralistic architectural scene, the practice remained loyal to the modernist tradition, though several projects of the 1980s had, to the dismay of many in the office, nodded to the passing fashion for post-modernism. On the eve of a new century, issues other than that of style, notably that of sustainability, came increasingly to the fore.

International projects

Britain was not the sole focus of Arup Associates' work. The practice, like its parent Ove Arup & Partners, always had an international dimension. Perhaps it was no coincidence, given the South African connections of Dowson and Zunz, that the first major project beyond Britain was a 22-storey office building for IBM in Johannesburg, completed in 1975. Alistair Gourlay ran the project during a five-year sojourn there, working with Ove Arup & Partners' local office.

The Sussex Stand, Goodwood, 1987–90

There were some in the office who were unhappy with the principle of working under apartheid, but by the mid-1990s, when the practice was responsible for the new athletics stadium in the city, apartheid had been dismantled.

The Middle East was a fertile market for British practices from the 1960s on, but it was not necessarily receptive to innovation. A 1983 project for the Islamic Development Bank in Jeddah was dropped in favour of a routine tower. Don Ferguson, who led on that project, was also the lead director, working with Stuart Mercer, for the Diplomatic Quarter Sports Club in Riyadh, which the Saudi authorities were keen to develop as a model capital city. Foreign embassies were concentrated in a new diplomatic quarter located 7km west of the city centre. As part of the master plan, it was decided to develop a large (94,000m²) sports and social centre open to all foreign diplomats and containing swimming pools, gymnasia, squash courts and sports pitches, along with a clubhouse and restaurant. Although the facility, completed in 1985, was designed for the exclusive use of non-Saudi nationals, Saudi Arabia's reactionary stance on the segregation of the sexes had to be observed, so that men and women used separate entrances and all sports activities were contained in screened enclosures. The complex was consequently designed as a series of walled spaces, concrete framed and stone clad, disposed along a pedestrian route extending 800m across the site and reflecting a Saudi tradition of

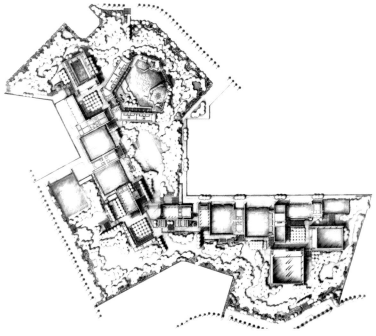

Diplomatic Quarter Sports Club, Riyadh: plan

Diplomatic Quarter Sports Club, Riyadh, 1981–4

solid structures designed to baffle sunlight and extreme heat. The clubhouse and restaurant were placed at the hub of the site, with two arms containing sports halls and gymnasia to the east and the swimming pools and squash courts to the north.

In structural terms, the Sports Club was quite straightforward: a family of concrete-framed buildings using a generic construction system with precast roof beams supported by primary beams and columns and solid stone-faced walls. The most impressive internal spaces were the covered pool and large sports hall, with roof spans of 24m. The greatest challenge of the project was environmental, coping with the extreme climate of the desert and the lack of water. Reverse heat pumps, warming the water in the mild Saudi winter and cooling it in summer, were installed in the outdoor pool. Solar collectors provided hot water for the changing rooms.

Competition and controversy

During the 1980s, the practice had boomed, with the commissions for Finsbury Avenue, Broadgate and Stockley Park bringing in fee income on an unprecedented level, but even then, there were worrying signs that its standing as one of the leading British practices was under challenge. Foggo had been bitterly disappointed, given the success of Arup Associates' Chatham project for Lloyd's of London, by Lloyd's decision to award the commission for its new City building to Richard Rogers (who was backed by a team from Ove Arup & Partners under Ted Happold and Peter Rice). Opened in 1986, the Lloyd's Building confirmed Rogers's position as a leading player in London.

In 1982, Arup Associates was on an invited shortlist to design the new BBC Radio Centre in Portland Place – but the commission went to Norman Foster, only for the project to be cancelled in 1985.

Also in 1982, the practice was on the final shortlist of three (with SOM and Ahrends, Burton & Koralek) for the proposed extension to the National Gallery.[1] The brief was, awkwardly, to combine new galleries with an office development, the latter funding the former. Famously, ABK won the competition, but their project was abandoned following an intervention in 1984 by the Prince of Wales, who pronounced the winning scheme to be 'like a monstrous carbuncle on the face of a much-loved and elegant friend'. There was a suspicion that he had become confused and was referring to the proposal by Richard Rogers, which had not been shortlisted, but the outcome was the same. The Gallery trustees, led by Lord Annan, lost their nerve and caved in, abandoning the competition. (Dowson thought that Annan had been privately lobbying for the selection of SOM's scheme.) When the Gallery finally got its extension, funded by the Sainsbury family, it was, externally, a weak exercise in post-modernism by the American practice Venturi Scott Brown. But the Prince was to impact even more on Arup Associates.

The Paternoster project

The area north of St Paul's Cathedral, including the historic Paternoster Square, had been completely levelled by wartime bombing. In 1961, redevelopment of the area began to a master plan by Lord Holford, which Pevsner thought 'outstandingly well-conceived'.[2] The architecture was by Trehearne & Norman, with a 16-storey tower and a series of lower blocks around open courtyards that Pevsner found 'inviting'. Few shared his opinion, however, and the countless tourists visiting the Cathedral gave the development a wide berth. Within 15 years of its completion, plans were in formation to redevelop the area once more. Property developer Mountleigh acquired the site and commissioned Stuart Lipton to manage a high-level ideas competition to secure an appropriate scheme. In 1987, a shortlist of architectural practices was announced, including Foster, Rogers, Stirling, Arata Isozaki, SOM, Richard MacCormac – and Arup Associates. The 'commercial' practices that had dominated the City for three decades were conspicuously excluded. The shortlisted proposals were exhibited in the crypt of St Paul's that summer. But also on show was a radically different proposal, by the young classicist John Simpson. Simpson's scheme had the support of the Prince of Wales, who had been shown the seven shortlisted schemes and, speaking in December 1987, declared that he was deeply depressed that none of them had risen to the occasion.[3]

Several months earlier, it had been announced that the scheme by Arup Associates was the competition winner and that the practice had been commissioned to develop its master plan. The Arup scheme, still a strategy rather than a final design, was shown at St Paul's in summer 1988, alongside a fully developed scheme by Simpson, which was backed by a handsome model and beautiful coloured perspectives by Carl Laubin that attracted public and media interest.

Writing in the *Architectural Review*, Francis Duffy commented that 'Arup Associates' winning submission persuaded the assessors by its strength and clarity of purpose. It responded directly to St Paul's and distinguished in architectural terms, as others did not, between what was to be permanent and what could be transient'.[4] Arup Associates' fully developed scheme was put on exhibition in December 1988, and included buildings designed by the practices of Richard MacCormac and Michael & Patty Hopkins – a welcome move to inject an element of diversity into the project. When the practice was approached to submit proposals in 1986, Foggo's Group 2 was immediately brought in, with a lead role given to Crispin Wride, who had been recruited to the group to replace Rab Bennetts.

Wride recalls that Dowson, who had been instrumental in the establishment of a Paternoster Committee, chaired by Lord St John (then chairman of the Royal Fine Art Commission), thought it essential to establish a wider project team.

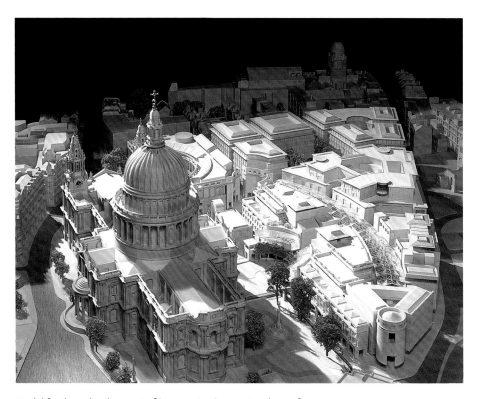

Model for the redevelopment of Paternoster Square, London, 1987

Already suspicious of the Prince's motives, given his role in the National Gallery debacle, Dowson felt that the Prince's Mansion House speech, 'with its unbalanced hyperbole, made any subsequent or sensible discussion impossible'. Debate about the merits of the selected scheme had been expected, but in the event, 'prejudiced opportunism at the expense of ethics marked the exercise'.[5] Moreover, in October 1988, the Prince had presented a television programme, 'HRH Prince Of Wales: A Vision of Britain', subsequently developed as a book, in which the Arup scheme was condemned as 'an exercise in watered-down classicism … A rather half-hearted, grudging attempt to accommodate public concern about the national importance to this great site'.[6] A presentation of the scheme to the Prince at Kensington Palace was a less than cordial occasion.

The politics of Paternoster Square obscured the fact that the Arup Associates scheme, in contrast to those by Foster and Rogers, was thoroughly contextual. It provided not only around 93,000m² of offices and 28,000m² of retailing and restaurants/cafés, but also 21,000m² of public spaces. A piazza was proposed to the west of St Paul's. To the north of the Cathedral, a new Cathedral Close would contain shops, bars and restaurants, with the historic Temple Bar, removed from the City in the 1870s, restored and given pride of place in a new square. The principal office and retail development was placed further north and planned around an arcaded street, providing a pedestrian route from Cheapside to Ludgate Hill. Beyond, to the west, a market square was proposed, 'to provide space for sitting and relaxing, a market, and the day to day activities of the City'.[7] Buildings by Hopkins and MacCormac were to be located around the square. No building on the site would exceed eight storeys in height and all would be faced in brick or stone. The essence of the scheme was 'the creation of a network of new public spaces on the site'. For some critics, entranced by the more radical approach of other architects, the scheme had post-modernist undertones. The colonnaded crescent addressing the western piazza seemed a formal device that recalled the Lloyds Bank headquarters in Bristol. But the columns were steel and part of a rational structural strategy, not applied ornament.

The development of the Paternoster project was complicated by the sale of the site in 1987 to a Venezuelan property group. Two years later, the site was sold again to a partnership of Greycoat with the American Park Tower group. The Arup scheme was abandoned and a new master plan commissioned, with John Simpson and Terry Farrell leading the new team. In the end, redevelopment of the site did not begin until 2000, with William Whitfield as master-planner. For Arup Associates, the saga of Paternoster Square was a dispiriting experience, denying the practice the chance to make its mark on the very heart of the City. Ironically, the scheme finally built, supposedly responding to Prince Charles's call for 'some sacrifice of profit … for generosity of vision', provided around 25 per cent more commercial space than the Arup scheme.

Forbes Mellon Library, Clare College, Cambridge

The 1980s saw post-modernism emerge as a significant force in British architecture, as even practices with a notable modernist past drifted into what some
old hands saw as an aberration. (For the veteran modernist master Berthold
Lubetkin, post-modernism was the architectural equivalent of Fascism.) There
was little sympathy for the new fashion at Arup Associates, though there were
projects – such as the Legal & General headquarters building in Surrey (*see*
Chapter 3), completed in 1988 – that reflected an overt interest in history.

Sugden recalled that there was 'great disagreement in the office' about the
designs for the new library at Clare College, Cambridge, completed in 1986.
Dowson had been an undergraduate at Clare and naturally took a close interest
in the project, working on it with Richard Frewer and James Burland. The siting
of the Forbes Mellon Library was itself controversial, located in the centre of the
College's Memorial Court, completed in 1936 to designs by Sir Giles Gilbert Scott
and framing views to the monumental University Library, by the same architect.
The Thirties Society strongly opposed the scheme, and *Private Eye*'s 'Piloti' lam-
basted 'a lame octagonal design with illiterate Classical details in a feeble attempt

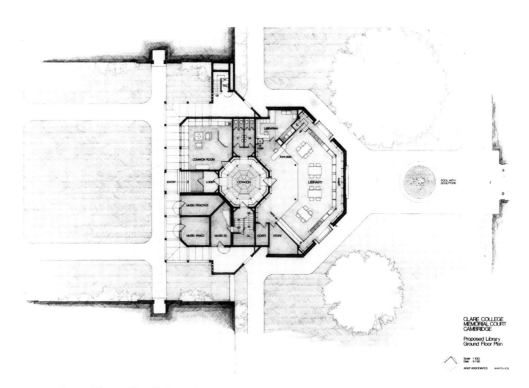

Forbes Mellon Library, Clare College, Cambridge: plan

to respect Scott's subtle neo-Georgian' that would block 'the most spectacular 20th century vista in Cambridge'.[8] The local authority planning committee was divided 3–3 when it came to a planning application. The matter was referred to the Secretary of State, and the support of the Royal Fine Art Commission was doubtless a factor in securing approval. The brief for the project was to combine a new undergraduate library with a recital room and musical rehearsal rooms and was skilfully addressed. The external treatment is more problematic: mostly in the manner of Lutyens, but with a post-modernist take on Brunelleschi forming the entrance elevation located, rather perversely, to the west. Nicholas Ray compared the building to Dowson's Leckhampton House, commenting that 'what has been lost is the appealing clarity of expression which seems, in retrospect, to have been a reflection of a less complicated and more optimistic world'.[9]

The Forbes Mellon Library, Clare Hall, 1982–6: view from the main entrance to the quad

The Forbes Mellon Library: entrance

International Garden Festival Hall, Liverpool

If the context of a Cambridge college generated a rather tortuous dialogue with history, which lacked the subtlety of Philip Dowson's earlier Oxbridge projects, neither history nor context were issues when it came to building on a derelict site on the fringes of Liverpool. In 1981, the Thatcher Government had established the Merseyside Development Corporation with a brief to regenerate the former docklands along the Mersey. Planning powers were taken away from Labour-controlled local authorities and vested in the Corporation. In 1984, Liverpool's docklands became the site for the International Garden Festival, the brainwave of Environment Secretary Michael Heseltine, which was to become a model for other garden festivals around the country. Arup Associates won the commission for a Festival Hall in competition – others on the shortlist included Terry Farrell and Nicholas Grimshaw. The hall was intended to be retained after the closure of the festival and used as a sports hall, an ongoing amenity for the local community. The Arup team included Richard Frewer, Ian Taylor, Mick Brundle and Terry Raggett, and the result was a building that married late 20th-century technology with the rational elegance of 19th-century glasshouse design. As Frewer admitted somewhat ruefully on the completion of the hall, the project '[has] acted as a focus for political mud-slinging for the last 18 months, and most of the journalists who have written of it during its construction have been determined that it was a political stunt which they appeared to hope would be a literal and proverbial wash-out'.[10]

The site for the festival had been used as a municipal rubbish dump for two decades, and the reclamation of the polluted land was a challenging task. The brief for the Festival Hall was relatively straightforward: three spaces, which could be used separately or combined as one, were required. One was to act as a conservatory and be largely glazed. But, as Frewer commented, 'the real problems of the brief related to satisfying the needs of the sports complex'.[11] Accommodation for track sports, squash courts, a swimming pool and a multipurpose sports hall with seating for 4,000 spectators were elements

Festival Hall, Liverpool Garden Festival, 1982–4 (now demolished): interior

of the brief, suggesting that the building should be significantly larger than the structure required for the Garden Festival. While the needs of the festival could be met by a temporary structure, the proposed ongoing use required a building with a long lifespan. A further challenge was the need to have the building ready for the opening of the festival on 2 May 1984 – the competition rules had allowed the practices involved only eight weeks to prepare designs and only a year was allowed for construction.

In many respects, however, the project was one that Arup Associates were uniquely equipped to tackle – it was 'a particularly clear example of architecture and engineering being of equal importance within the hypothesis'.[12] The response to the complex brief was a design for a 'loose fit' building, an adaptable envelope. On one level, this had to be a very simple building, economical to construct and easy to maintain, but equally, it would serve as a symbol of the festival – and of the regeneration process of which the latter was a part – so should be memorable in form and an addition to Liverpool's distinguished architectural heritage. There were obvious precedents for a lightweight garden building, such as the Crystal Palace and the Palm House at Kew. The completed building could equally be seen as resembling a grounded airship. Its form was that of a dome, sliced in two, its two halves connected by a vaulted hall, the entire ($7500m^2$) space being column-free. The domes were clad in profiled aluminium sheet, the central hall in polycarbonate sheet carried on steel trusses.

The festival closed on 14 October 1984, but the planned conversion of the hall never happened. Liverpool City Council had come under Labour control in 1983 and thereafter maintained a hostile stance to the festival, seeing it as a Thatcherite project. The site fell into dereliction and a planned housing development there was abandoned. The Festival Hall was demolished in 2006, a tragic waste of a building with a potentially long and useful life and a notably rational fusion of architecture and engineering. In 2015, the Council bought the site, aiming to turn it into 'a world-class cultural destination'. It was reported to be in 'a sorry state'.[13]

Goodwood Racecourse

The setting of 'Glorious Goodwood', high on the Sussex Downs, is unrivalled among British racecourses. A new grandstand designed by the Lobb Partnership with engineer Jan Bobrowski had been completed in 1980 and Dowson had acted as consultant for the project at the request of the Duke of Richmond. Replacing a grandstand of 1904, described by Ian Nairn as 'like an enlarged Oxford college barge',[14] the Lobb stand is a rather heavy and overbearing masted structure of concrete that is at odds with the spirit of a racecourse that King Edward VII allegedly described as 'really a garden party, with racing tacked on'. In 1987, Dowson was approached to undertake a master plan for

Sussex Stand, Goodwood Racecourse: tented roof

Sussex Stand, Goodwood Racecourse: view from course, with, to right, the earlier stand by the Lobb Partnership

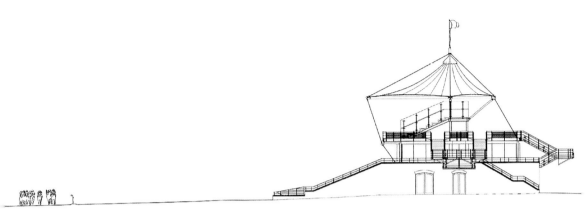

Sussex Stand, Goodwood Racecourse: section

the future development of the whole site. Better facilities for race-goers, not only the elite members and the increasing number of corporate patrons but equally the less affluent punters, were badly needed. There was also a move to relocate the winning post, straightening the course to reduce the likelihood of injuries to horses, though the head-on view from the members' enclosure had to be retained.

The first phase of development included provision of a new members' restaurant in the Head On Stand, along with the moving of the winning post and associated changes to routes within the course. The key feature of the second phase, on which David Thomas worked with Terry Raggett, was the Sussex Stand. Tents and marquees were a prominent feature of the course during the racing season, and the designs for the Sussex Stand, completed in 1990, take their cue from this tradition of lightweight structures. The use of a fabric structure carried on masts was not entirely novel: Michael Hopkins had used one at the Mound Stand at Lord's Cricket Ground a few years earlier. The Lobb Grandstand had placed corporate dining spaces above seating for ordinary race-goers. The Sussex Stand put public seating (for 'Tattersall's' customers) above the hospitality suites. Rab Bennetts commented that the Sussex Stand was 'a somewhat quirky design involving a seemingly disproportionate amount of effort for just three structural bays. Subjectively, the slightly top-heavy proportions of the building make it look as if it should originally have been several times as long'.[15] In fact, an entire bay was removed from the initial designs on cost grounds, while the substantial structure was necessitated by the stand's location high on the Downs and subject to strong winds. The final phase of development, in line with the Arup master plan, was entrusted to Michael Hopkins & Partners and included the reconfiguration of the parade ground and promenade and the provision of new refreshment facilities in tented pavilions.

City of Manchester Stadium

The Sussex Stand suggested that Arup Associates was well equipped to design larger stadia, and sports buildings have more recently become a major element in the practice's workload. The King Abdullah Sports City in Saudi Arabia and the Singapore Sports Hub are examples, both very large in scale. The largest of Arup Associates' sports projects in Britain is the City of Manchester Stadium, now Etihad Stadium, initially conceived in 1992 as part of Manchester's unsuccessful bids to stage the 1996 and 2000 Olympic Games. The scheme was taken forward first as Manchester's submission for the National Stadium (which went to Wembley) and then, with a reduced seating capacity, as part of the city's winning bid for the 2002 Commonwealth Games.

The site was in east Manchester and had previously been occupied by a colliery. While the original Olympic stadium designs provided for 80,000 seats, the brief for the Commonwealth Games was for no more than 38,000. A major consideration in the development of the scheme was the decision that, after the games, the stadium would become the home of Manchester City Football Club, which was to move from its very inadequate ground at Maine Road, Moss Side, with a further 10,000 seats added. Adaptability was therefore a fundamental consideration. The strategy was that, after the games, the athletics track would be removed, the pitch lowered by 6m and 13 additional rows of seating installed. The temporary stand built to allow space for the running track would be demolished and the final element in the run of permanent stands slotted in.

The initial designs for the stadium, which formed the basis of the completed project, were produced by James Burland, who had rejoined Arup Associates in 1990 after a few years' break, when he had worked with Philip Cox in Australia on a number of stadia. His first project following his return was an unbuilt scheme (1992) that formed part of Berlin's unsuccessful bid for the 2000 Olympics. There, working with Terry Raggett, Burland developed designs for a stadium with seating under a cable-stayed roof, and stairs and lifts located in a series of peripheral towers. The 38,000-seat athletics stadium in Johannesburg was completed in 1995 and featured another roof structure supported on steel masts and cables. Provision was made for expanding the capacity to 55,000 spectators with a further phase of construction on the eastern side of the site.

The Manchester stadium further developed the key ideas of the Berlin and Johannesburg projects. Burland and Raggett's proposal was for a roof structure independent of the stadium bowl, with masts on top of towers incorporating services and ramps – rather than stairs – for access. Burland further refined the designs with engineer Tristram Carfrae of Ove Arup & Partners, with whom he had worked in Australia, producing an even more economical and adaptable scheme, using a lightweight tension structure. The Manchester stadium was seen as a classic beacon of regeneration, headlining the renewal of post-industrial East Manchester, and the structural design addresses this agenda triumphantly.

Etihad Stadium, Manchester, 1993–2000: view across the pitch

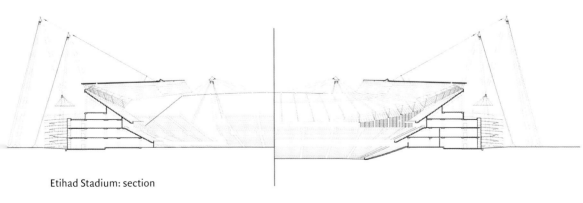

Etihad Stadium: section

The lightweight roof, constructed of aluminium and polycarbonate, covering the stands is carried on 12 cable-stayed masts, up to 75m high. Spiral ramps, rather than steps, contained in eight service towers, provide access to the seating – and the gentle gradient makes them accessible to wheelchair users. But the most important feature of the stadium is that it provides an outstanding experience for spectators, with excellent sightlines and real atmosphere – the architects envisaged 'an intimate, even intimidating gladiatorial arena'.[16] The successful adaptation of the stadium to football use, at relatively low cost, stands in stark contrast to the saga of London's 2012 Olympic Stadium.

Contextuality, 'radical traditionalism' and sustainability

Where large sports stadia were concerned, the issue of contextuality barely arose. But it was to the fore in a number of projects emerging from the office during the mid- and late 1990s. A notable example was the Gro at Newtown in mid Wales, commissioned by an electronics company and incorporating both headquarters offices and research and development space. The site, on the edge of the small market town, was adjacent to a local landmark, Gro Tump, with the mound of a lost medieval castle. The mound became the focus of the development, with a building sunk into the ground to the west and rising above ground level to the east, where a retaining wall provided protection from possible flooding. The building was divided into two zones, with research and development facilities on the west linked by bridges across a central circulation zone to offices and meeting rooms on the east, and a separate circular pavilion containing a staff restaurant and kitchens. The unaffected elegance of the building makes it a model for the development of new industries in rural areas.[17]

'Radical traditionalism' was one description applied to some of the projects of the 1990s. Arup Associates had proved its ability to work with traditional materials in earlier projects, including the Babergh District Council Offices and the reconstruction of Bedford School. The tennis pavilion at Wentworth Golf Club in Surrey, completed in 1990, was equally a straightforward exercise in the use of timber. The club had appointed Arup Associates in 1989 to develop a master plan for the development of new facilities for golf and tennis on its extensive site. The proposed golf clubhouse, a three-storey building sunk into the landscape taking advantage of views across greens and adjacent woods, remained unbuilt. But the pavilion serving the tennis courts, a more modest single-storey structure, was realised: an exemplary example of timber design in Douglas fir with an exposed steel roof structure supporting a slate roof. Entirely undemonstrative, the building is a good example of a contemporary architect – the project architect was Rodney Tan – reinterpreting a Victorian tradition.

Etihad Stadium: exterior with masts supporting the roof

The Gro, Newtown, Wales, 1993–9

The Arup Campus at Solihull – developed in two phases, with three two-storey, timber-clad office pavilions completed respectively in 2001 and 2007 – was a classic example of the theme of radical traditionalism, a bold reinterpretation of the vernacular of rural barns and sheds. The development, located in a business park on the edge of the town and designed with its relationship to the sloping site as a key consideration, was commissioned by British Land for occupation by the Arup Group, housing a number of teams that previously had been scattered across several locations in the West Midlands. But alongside fresh thinking, the project embodied significant elements of continuity in Arup Associates' work. James Burland, who worked on the first phase of the campus designs with Terry Raggett, Peter Warburton and Michael Beaven, confessed that the project was 'hugely important to me, as I wanted to show how the new work was linked to the history'.[18]

Above: Arup Campus, Solihull, 1999–2007: interior of offices
Following page: Arup Campus, Solihull: exterior

The Arup Building Group's work at Duxford was one significant source of inspiration, with the controlled use of natural light a key concern. The issue of sustainability had not been to the fore in the early 1950s, but the Duxford section adapted well to a natural ventilation strategy, with giant roof pods acting as chimneys to drive a stack effect and draw fresh air through the office spaces; they also channel daylight into the centre of the office floors. The controlled use of natural light had been a key feature of early Arup industrial buildings. Opening windows, solar shading, and an exposed concrete structure providing thermal mass were further ingredients in this strategy. 'Green' design was to become a major theme in Arup Associates' work around the end of the 20th century. A team led by Burland was responsible for the 'Solar Showcase' designed for British Petroleum in 1998 to demonstrate the potential of solar energy and to coincide with a meeting of G8 leaders held in Birmingham that year. In effect a small pavilion, with a sloping south wall clad in photovoltaic cells, the structure was later relocated to a business park in South Wales. Burland's departure from the practice was another turning point in its history, with leadership passing into new hands.

In 2013, Arup Associates celebrated its 50th birthday, declaring its work to be about 'shared values and commitment to pioneering design through integrated working', with 'a deliberate focus on how architecture and engineering can contribute to a sense of common good'.[19] Virtually all the architectural practices that had been its competitors in the early years had ceased to exist: Arup Associates was, and remains, a great survivor. For Ove Arup, one dictum was of supreme importance: 'good design should embody a sensible way of building'. 'I want the warm humanity of art to permeate the cold economics of building', he insisted.[20] The huge body of work produced by the architectural practice he founded has done a great deal to fulfil that vision.

Notes

Introduction

1 'Art and Architecture', in Tonks, N (ed) 2012 *Ove Arup: Philosophy of Design, Essays 1942–1981*. Munich and London: Prestel, 100.

2 Ibid, 143.

3 Saint, A 2007 *Architect and Engineer: A Study in Sibling Rivalry*. New Haven and London: Yale University Press, 365.

4 Sturgis, T nd 'Memories of the 1960s at Arup Associates'. Unpublished typescript sent to the author, unpag.

5 Dowson, P 1977 'Offices'. *Arup Journal* **12**/4, Dec 1977, 2.

6 Davies, C 1989 'Fast building: milestone or millstone?' (Interview with Peter Foggo). *Architects' Journal* **190**/15, 11 Oct 1989, 79.

1 Origins and industrial buildings

1 Saint, A 2007 *Architect and Engineer: A Study in Sibling Rivalry*. New Haven, CT and London: Yale University Press, 365.

2 Jones, P 2006 *Ove Arup: Masterbuilder of the Twentieth Century*. New Haven, CT and London: Yale University Press, 16.

3 'The Engineer Looks Back' in Tonks, N (ed) 2012 *Ove Arup: Philosophy of Design, Essays 1942–1981*. Munich and London: Prestel, 210.

4 Ibid, 7.

5 Brawne, M 1983 *Arup Associates: The Biography of an Architectural Practice*. London: Lund Humphries, 31.

6 Zunz, J 2006 Obituary of Ronald Hobbs. *Arup Bulletin*, Mar 2006.

7 Dowson, P 2010 *Fragments and Ambushes*. Privately published, 93.

8 Ibid, 112.

9 *Architectural Review* **121**/723, Apr 1957, 231.

10 *Architectural Design* **38**/11, Nov 1968, 520. The issue contains an extended essay by Sugden on 'The anatomy of the factory', illustrating recent factory buildings in Italy, Switzerland, Japan and the USA.

11 Pevsner, N 1970 *Cambridgeshire* (The Buildings of England), 2 edn. Harmondsworth: Penguin, 334. (New 2014 edn, New Haven and London: Yale University Press 474.)

12 Derek Sugden in conversation with the author, 19 Nov 2014.

13 *Architects' Journal* **137**/1, 2 Jan 1963, 33.

14 *Architects' Journal* **136**/9, 29 Aug 1962, 552.

15 Derek Sugden in conversation with the author, 19 Nov 2014.

16 Dowson 2010, 130.

17 Ibid, 127.

18 Ibid.

19 All quotations in this section are taken from conversations with the author

20 *Architectural Review* **151**/904, Jun 1972, 360.

21 *Architects' Journal* **173**/2, 3 Jun 1981, 1057.

22 *Architects' Journal* **163**/16, 21 Apr 1976, 799.

23 Ibid, 804.

24 King, D nd 'Working at Arups'. Unpublished text, unpag.

2 University buildings

1 Letter to Prof George Kane, 21 Sep 1966, Somerville College Archives.

2 Dowson, P 2010 *Fragments and Ambushes.* Privately published, 76.

3 Fair, A 2014 '"Brutalism among the ladies": Modern architecture at Somerville College, Oxford, 1947–67'. *Architectural History* **57**, 357–82, 386; *see also* Manuel, A (ed) 2013 *Breaking New Ground: A History of Somerville College as Seen Through Its Buildings.* Oxford: Somerville College, 43–7.

4 Pevsner, N and Sherwood, J 1974 *Oxfordshire* (The Buildings of England). Harmondsworth: Penguin, 66.

5 Building Committee minutes, Feb 1959, Somerville College Archives.

6 Arup report to Building Committee, 26 May 1959, Somerville College Archives.

7 Sturgis, T nd *Memories of the 1960s at Arup Associates.* Unpublished typescript sent to the author, unpag.

8 Taylor, N 1965 'Graduate housing: Corpus Christi College, Cambridge'. *Architectural Review* **137**/816, Feb 1965, 110.

9 Smith, D L nd (c 1961) *New Oxford: A Guide to the Modern City.* Oxford: University Design Society, unpag.

10 Dowson, P 1968 'A room of one's own'. *Architectural Design* **38**/4, Apr 1968, 164–72.

11 Philip Dowson in conversation with Elain Harwood, 21 Mar 2012.

12 Pevsner and Sherwood 1974, 252.

13 Box marked 'George Thomson Building', Corpus Christi College Archives.

14 Sturgis nd, unpag. I am grateful to Prof Peter Carolin of Corpus Christi College for arranging a visit to Leckhampton and for useful comments on the project.

15 Hughes, N, Lewison, G and Wesley, T 1964 *Cambridge New Architecture.* Cambridge: self-published, 100.

16 Banham, R 1968 'Arts in Society, Cambridge Mark II'. *New Society* **313**, 26 Sep 1968, 454–5.

17 For an account of the building from a college perspective and its recent restoration *see* Carolin, P 2014 'A fabulous place to live in'. *The Letter* (Corpus Christi College) **93**, 2014, 24–9.

18 Cited in Tyack, G 2005 *Modern Architecture in an Oxford College: St John's College, 1945–2005.* Oxford: OUP, 47. Tyack's book provides a comprehensive account of the development process of the Sir Thomas White Building and of the other post-war buildings of St John's College.

19 Muniment lxxxi, 170, St John's College Archives.

20 Letter to Philip Dowson, 19 Oct 1971, President's File, Box 179, St John's College Archives.

21 Dowson 2010, 139.

22 Letter dated 4 Aug 1971, President's File, Box 179, St John's College Archives. Dowson was working on a new headquarters for IBM in Johannesburg, won by Arup Associates in competition in 1970.

23 Sturgis nd, unpag.

24 Muniment lxxxi, 170, St John's College Archives.

25 Letter to Philip Dowson, 19 Oct 1971, President's File, Box 179, St John's College Archives.

26 Sturgis nd, unpag.

27 'Oxford: new buildings at Keble and St John's'. *Architectural Review* **162**/970, Dec 1977, 360.

28 Dowson 1968, 164.

29 Dowson, P 1979 'St John's College: Thomas White Building'. *Arup Journal* **14**/1, Apr 1979, 2. James Lees-Milne, not usually an enthusiast for modern architecture, found the St John's buildings 'sensitive,

original, and yet conformist': Lees-Milne, J 1998 *Through Wood and Dale: Diaries 1975–1978*. London: John Murray, 67.

30 Brawne, M 1983 *Arup Associates: The Biography of an Architectural Practice*. London: Lund Humphries, 98.

31 Harwood, E 2015 *Space, Hope and Brutalism*. New Haven, CT: Yale University Press, 245; Foster, A 2005 *Birmingham* (Pevsner Architectural Guide). New Haven, CT and London: Yale University Press, 250.

32 Brawne 1983, 98.

33 Tyack, G 1998 *Oxford: An Architectural Guide*. Oxford: OUP, 320.

34 Ibid.

35 Derek Sugden in conversation with the author, 18 Dec 2014.

36 Bradley, S and Pevsner, N 2014 *Cambridgeshire* (The Buildings of England). New Haven, CT and London: Yale University Press, 256.

37 Calder, B 2013 'Representing science: the architecture of the New Museums Site, Cambridge, 1952–71' in Harwood, E, Powers, A and Saumarez Smith, O (eds) 2013 *Oxford and Cambridge* (Twentieth Century Architecture 11). London: Twentieth Century Society, 177.

38 Crosby, T 1974 'New Museums Building'. *Architectural Review* 155/924, Feb 1974, 75–6.

39 Whyte, W 2013 'A pastiche or a packing case: building in twentieth century Oxford and Cambridge' in Harwood *et al* 2013, 27.

3 Office buildings

1 Brawne, M 1983 *Arup Associates: The Biography of an Architectural Practice*. London: Lund Humphries, 65.

2 Ibid, 66.

3 Girouard, M 1972 *Architectural Review* 151/902, Apr 1972, 223–32, 230.

4 Gordon, A 1972 'Designing for survival: the President introduces his long life/loose fit/low energy study'. RIBA *Journal* 79/9, Sep 1972, 374–6.

5 Blackmore, C 1990 *The Client's Tale: The Role of the Client in Building Buildings*. London: RIBA Publications, 47.

6 Price, S 2001 'Different models of interdisciplinary collaboration' in Spence, R, Macmillan, S and Kirby, P (eds) 2001 *Interdisciplinary Design in Practice*. London: Thomas Telford, 82.

7 Blackmore 1990, 48.

8 Tony Marriott, interviewed by the author, 9 Mar 2016.

9 Foyle, A and Pevsner, N 2011 *Somerset: North and Bristol* (The Buildings of England). New Haven, CT and London: Yale University Press, 416.

10 Tony Marriott, interviewed by the author, 9 Mar 2016.

11 Hawkes, D 1996 *The Environmental Tradition: Studies in the Architecture of Environment*. London: E&FN Spon, 152–3.

12 *Architects' Journal* 170/7, 15 Aug 1979, 337.

13 *Architectural Review* 169/26, Jul 1979, 14–15.

14 Davies, C and Pearman, H 1985 'One Finsbury Avenue'. *Designers' Journal* 6, Jan 1985, 29.

15 Carolin, P 1983 'Racing up the Avenue'. *Architects' Journal*, 178/34/35, 24/31 Aug 1983, 65–7, 67.

16 Buchanan, P 1985 'Urban Arups'. *Architectural Review*, 177/1059, May 1985, 18–30, 30.

17 Lipton, S 1994 'Something in the City'. *Building Design* 1184/5, 12 Aug 1994, 12.

18 Stuart Lipton in conversation with the author, 3 Sep 2015. The idea of a screen façade, in this case in bronze, was developed further in Foggo Associates' No. 60 Queen Victoria Street, *see Architects' Journal* 211/6, 10 Feb 2000, 27–34.

19 Richard MacCormac wrote that Broadgate
    was 'an exemplar for the modern city and
    a reminder in these disaggregated times
    that the well-being of the individual is
    deeply linked to the idea of civic order'
    (*Building Design* **1184**/5, 12 Aug 1994, 12).
20 I am immensely grateful to Rab Bennetts
    for sharing his paper, 'An architect's
    perspective' (unpublished paper dated
    Oct 2011), and his other memories of
    working with Peter Foggo.
21 Huntley, C 1987 'The future according to
    Broadgate'. *Building* **252**/7495, 8 May 1987, 56.
22 Michael Lowe, interviewed by the author,
    5 Oct 2015.
23 For a retrospective overview of Stockley
    Park, *see* 'Offices', *Building Design Magazine*
    23, Dec 2008, 16–21.
24 *Building Design* **1184**/5, 12 Aug 1994, 14;
    Bennetts, R 2011 'Broadgate: an architect's
    perspective'. *C20 Magazine*, Autumn 2011, 8.
25 For a detailed account of the project, *see*
    Arup Journal, Autumn 1991, 3–10.
26 Foyle and Pevsner 2011, 315; Aldous, T
    2000 *C20: Bristol's Twentieth Century
    Buildings*. Bristol: Redcliffe Press, 83.
27 Arup, O 1966 'Art and architecture: the
    architect–engineer relationship' (Gold
    Medal address). RIBA *Journal* **73**/8, 7 Aug
    1966, 359.

4 Public buildings and conversions

1 For an overview of the decade, *see*
   Harwood, E and Powers, A 2012 'From
   downtown to diversity: revisiting the
   1970s' in Harwood, E and Powers, A (eds)
   2012 *The Seventies* (Twentieth Century
   Architecture **10**). London: Twentieth
   Century Society, 9–36. *See also* Wartnaby, S
   2012 'An exemplary 1970s building: Gun
   Wharf, Chatham' *in ibid*, 131–5.
2 For the Long Melford house, *see* Cantacuzino, S 1964 *Modern Houses of the World*.
   London: Studio Vista, 69–71 and *Country
   Life* **137**/3547, 25 Feb 1965, 432–3. For the
   post-1994 restoration by Hugh Pilkington,
   see 'Conservation, restoration and
   addition: work at Long Wall, Long
   Melford, Suffolk' in Powers, A (ed) 2000
   Post-War Houses (Twentieth Century
   Architecture **4**), 47–50.
3 Derek Sugden in conversation with the
   author, 18 Dec 2014.
4 *Arup Journal* **1**/4, Jun 1967, 7 – the issue
   contains a full account of the project. *See
   also* Edwards, D 2013 *The House that Britten
   Built: How the Aldeburgh Festival Brought Music
   to the Maltings*. Aldeburgh: Aldeburgh Music.
5 Edwards 2013, 33.
6 *Arup Journal* **1**/4, Jun 1967, 1–28, 17.
7 Derek Sugden in conversation with the
   author, 18 Dec 2014.
8 Williamson, E, Riches, A and Higgs, M
   1990 *Glasgow* (The Buildings of Scotland).
   Harmondsworth: Penguin, 208–9.
9 Brawne, M 1983 *Arup Associates: The
   Biography of an Architectural Practice*. London:
   Lund Humphries, 129.
10 *Arup Journal* **2**, 2002, 43–7.

5 Later works

1 For an analysis of the shortlisted schemes
   see Architects' Journal **176**/43, 27 Oct 1982,
   38–40.
2 Pevsner, N and Cherry, B 1973 *London
   Volume 1: The Cities of London and Westminster*
   (The Buildings of England). Harmondsworth: Penguin, 285.
3 The comment was made in a speech at the
   Mansion House on 1 Dec 1987. For the text
   of the speech, *see* Jencks, C 1988 *The Prince,
   the Architects and New Wave Monarchy*.
   London: Academy Editions, 47–9.

4 Duffy, F 1988 'Paternoster'. *Architectural Review* **183**/1091, Jan 1988, 19–20.

5 Dowson, P 2010 *Fragments and Ambushes.* Privately published, 216.

6 HRH The Prince of Wales 1989 *A Vision of Britain: A Personal View of Architecture.* London: Doubleday, 72.

7 The scheme is described in detail in Burdett, R and Hadidian, M 1987 *Paternoster Square: Urban Design Competition.* London: Arup Associates.

8 *Private Eye* **539**, 13 Aug 1982, 7.

9 Ray, N 1994 *Cambridge Architecture: A Concise Guide.* Cambridge: CUP, 97.

10 Frewer, R 1984 'The Festival Hall, International Garden Festival Liverpool '84'. *Arup Journal* **19**/3, Oct 1984, 2–4.

11 Ibid, 3.

12 Ibid, 4.

13 *Liverpool Echo*, 9 Aug 2015.

14 Nairn, I and Pevsner, N 1965 *Sussex* (The Buildings of England). Harmondsworth: Penguin, 230. For the Lobb stand, *see Concrete Quarterly*, Oct/Dec 1980, 27–30.

15 Bennetts, R 1990 'Rational and romantic'. *Architecture Today* **11**, Sep 1990, 66–73 (73).

16 James Burland in an email to the author, 12 Jun 2016.

17 *Arup Journal*, **32**/1, Mar 1997, 15–17.

18 James Burland in an email to the author, 12 Jun 2016.

19 Powell, K 2013 *Arup Associates 50.* London: Arup Associates, 7.

20 Arup, O 1966 'Art and architecture: the architect–engineer relationship' (Gold Medal address). *RIBA Journal* **73**/8, 7 Aug 1966, 350–9, 359.

List of works

A select list of works by the Building Group, Ove Arup & Partners, 1955–63/ Arup Associates, 1963–2000

★   Substantially altered or partly demolished
★★   Demolished
★★★   Unbuilt
Bold type indicates works profiled in this book

1950
Aero Research Production Factory
Duxford, Cambridgeshire
Client: Aero Research Ltd
The Builder **180**/5630, 12 Jan 1951, 63–7

1953–5
Chemical Building Products Factory★★
Hemel Hempstead, Hertfordshire
Client: Chemical Building Products
Architect & Building News **211**/19, 16 May 1957, 624–9

1954–8
Araldite Research Laboratories★★
Duxford, Cambridgeshire
Client: CIBA Ltd
Architect & Building News **216**/16, 25 Nov 1959, 519–28
Architects' Journal **131**/3378, 14 Jan 1960, 79–88

1956
Chemical Building Products Paint Factory★★
Hemel Hempstead, Hertfordshire

Client: Chemical Building Products
Architects' Journal **124**/3235, 20 Dec 1956, 901–14

1957–9
Zander House
Monks Eleigh, Suffolk
Client: Mr and Mrs M Zander
McKean, C 1982 *Architectural Guide to Cambridge and East Anglia since 1920.* London: RIBA Publications, 106
Bettley, J and Pevsner, N 2015 *Suffolk West (The Buildings of England).* London and New Haven, CT: Yale University Press, 413

1957–61
Smith Kline & French Chemical Plant★★
Tonbridge, Kent
Client: Smith Kline & French

1957–61
Smith Kline & French Factory, Laboratories and Offices★★
Welwyn Garden City, Hertfordshire
Client: Smith Kline & French
Architects' Journal **140**/21, 18 Nov 1964, 1175–94

Briarcliff House, Farnborough, 1978–83: internal courtyard

1958–66
Margery Fry and Elizabeth Nuffield House and Vaughan House, Somerville College
Oxford
Client: Somerville College, Oxford
Architects' Journal **130**/3369, 12 Nov 1959, 495–6
Architectural Review **137**/816, Feb 1965, 110–13
Tyack, G 1998 *Oxford: An Architectural Guide.* Oxford: OUP, 317–18
Manuel, A (ed) 2013 *Breaking New Ground: A History of Somerville College as Seen Through Its Buildings.* Oxford: Somerville College, 43–7
Fair, A 2014 '"Brutalism among the ladies": Modern architecture at Somerville College, Oxford, 1947–67'. *Architectural History* **57**, 357–92

1959–62
York Borg Shipley Factory★★
Basildon, Essex
Client: York Borg Warner Ltd
Architects' Journal **137**/1, 2 Jan 1963, 33–42

1959–64
Point Royal Flats
Bracknell, Berkshire
Client: Bracknell Development Corporation
Listed at grade II in 1998
Architects' Journal **139**/20, 13 May 1964, 1099–112

1959–69
Nuclear Physics Building, University of Oxford
Oxford
Client: University of Oxford
Tyack, G 1998 *Oxford: An Architectural Guide.* Oxford: OUP, 320

1960–6
Evode Factory Buildings★★
Stafford, Staffordshire
Client: Evode Ltd
Architects' Journal **136**/9, 29 Aug 1962, 551–60
Industrial Architecture **5**, Nov 1962, 742–4
Architect & Building News **223**/11, 13 Mar 1963, 385–9

1960–64
CIBA Multipurpose Building★★
Duxford, Cambridgeshire
Client: CIBA Ltd
Architecture & Building **35**/5, May 1960, 188–91
Arup Journal, May 1966, 10

1961–4
George Thomson Building, Corpus Christi College
Cambridge
Client: Corpus Christi College, Cambridge
Listed at grade II in 1993
Architectural Review **137**/816, Feb 1965, 105–10
Architects' Journal **141**/11, 17 Mar 1965, 411–24
Architect & Building News **227**/13, 31 Mar 1965, 605–10
Architects' Journal **157**/11, 14 Mar 1973, 607–18
Carolin, P 2014 'A fabulous place to live in'. *The Letter* (Corpus Christi College) **93**, 24–9

1962–4
Williams House (Long Wall)
Listed at grade II in 1997
Acton, Long Melford, Suffolk
Client: Mr and Mrs B Williams
Cantacuzino, S 1964 *Modern Houses of the World.* London: Studio Vista, 69–71
Country Life **137**/3547, 25 Feb 1965, 432–3

1962–5
Swimming Pool★★
Walton-on-Thames, Surrey
Client: Walton-on-Thames Borough
Council
Deutsche Bauzeitung **1**, 1967, 18–21
Webb, B 1969 *Architecture in Britain Today*
(London: Hamlyn Publishing Group), 220–1
Nairn, I and Pevsner, N 1971 *Surrey* (The
Buildings of England) 2 edn, 497–8

1962–6
**Metallurgy and Minerals Building,
University of Birmingham★**
Birmingham
Client: University of Birmingham
Listed at grade II in 1993
Architectural Design **37**, 4 Apr 1967, 160–70
Architects' Journal **145**/15, 12 Apr 1967, 905–18
Foster, A 2005 *Birmingham* (Pevsner Architectural Guides). New Haven, CT and London:
Yale University Press, 250

1964–6
**University of Loughborough,
master plan**
Loughborough, Leicestershire
Client: University of Loughborough
Architect & Building News **229**/25, 22 Jun 1966,
1114–16
Architects' Journal **143**/25, 22 Jun 1966, 1510–13

1964–70
**Attenborough Tower (Arts and
Social Sciences Building), University
of Leicester**
Leicester
Client: University of Leicester
Architecture East Midlands **43**, Jul/Aug 1972, 37–41
Arup Journal **8**/4, Dec 1973, 15
Architecture Plus **2**, May/Jun 1974, 78–83

1964–70
**Muirhead Tower (Arts and Commerce
Building), University of Birmingham**
Birmingham
Client: University of Birmingham
A+U **4** (2), Feb 1974, 51–6

1964–71
**New Museums Building, University
of Cambridge**
Cambridge
Client: University of Cambridge
Architectural Review **155**/924, Feb 1974, 71–84
Calder, B 2013 'Representing science: the
architecture of the New Museums Site,
Cambridge, 1952–71' in Harwood, E, Powers,
A and Saumarez Smith, O (eds) 2013 *Oxford
and Cambridge* (Twentieth Century Architecture 11). London: Twentieth Century Society,
166–79

1965–6
Ove Arup & Partners Offices
South Queensferry, Edinburgh
Client: Ove Arup & Partners

1965–7
Wolfson Building, Somerville College
Oxford
Client: Somerville College, Oxford
Listed at grade II in 2009
Architectural Design **38**/4, Apr 1968, 164–72
Architect & Building News **233**/18, 1 May 1968,
650–7

1965–7
Snape Maltings Concert Hall
Snape, Suffolk
Client: Aldeburgh Festival
Arup Journal **4**/1, Jun 1967, 2–27
Architects' Journal **146**/11, 13 Sep 1967, 687–91
Architectural Review **142**/847, Sep 1967, 202–7

Edwards, D 2013 *The House that Britten Built:
How the Aldeburgh Festival Brought Music to the
Maltings*. Aldeburgh: Aldeburgh Music

1965–8
Civil Engineering Building,
University of Loughborough
Loughborough, Leicestershire
Client: University of Loughborough
Architect & Building News **229**/25, 22 Jun 1966,
1114–16
Architects' Journal **143**/25, 22 Jun 1966, 1510–13

1965–9
Zunz House
Wimbledon, London
Client: Mr and Mrs J Zunz
Listed at grade II in 2013
Architectural Review **152**/906, Aug 1972, 83–8

1965–71
**Oxford Mail and Times Offices
and Printing Plant**
Oxford
Client: Oxford Mail and Times
Architects' Journal **155**/14, 5 Apr 1972, 721–34
Architectural Review **151**/902, Apr 1972, 223–32

1966–8
Boulton House, Trinity Hall
Cambridge
Client: Trinity Hall, Cambridge
Architectural Review **146**/870, Aug 1969, 98–101

1966–9
IBM Computer Centre, phase 1
Havant, Hampshire
Client: IBM UK Ltd
Architecture **396**, Apr 1976, 102–4
Architectural Review **151**/899, Jan 1972, 4–24

House for Mr and Mrs Zunz, Wimbledon, 1965–9

1966–72
Penguin Books Offices and Warehouse
Harmondsworth, Middlesex
Client: Penguin Books Ltd
Architects' Journal **157**/21, 23 May 1973, 1245–60
Concrete Quarterly **98**, Jul/Sep 1973, 15–17

1966–76
Kensington Central Depot
Kensington, London
Client: Royal Borough of Kensington & Chelsea
Brick Bulletin, Oct 1976, 4–11
Baumeister **74**/12, Dec 1977, 1144–6

1967–74
Residential Building, University College, Oxford
Oxford
Client: University College, Oxford

1968–71
Horizon Factory
Nottingham
Client: Imperial Tobacco Group Ltd
Building **222**/6723, 31 Mar 1972, 32–5
Architectural Review **151**/904, Jun 1972, 353–64
Architects' Journal **157**/7, 14 Feb 1973, 395–400

1968–74
IBM Systems Assembly Plant, phases 1–3
Havant, Hampshire
Client: IBM UK Ltd
Architecture **396**, Apr 1976, 102–4

1969–72
IBM Distribution Centre
Havant, Hampshire
Client: IBM UK Ltd

1969–73
British Sugar Corporation Offices
Peterborough, Cambridgeshire
Client: British Sugar Corporation
RIBA Journal **82**/7–8, Jul/Aug 1975, 20
Architects' Journal **162**/41, 8 Oct 1975, 731–46

1969–75
IBM Building Johannesburg
Johannesburg, South Africa
Client: IBM
Architectural Review **169**/954, Aug 1976, 111–18

1969–76
Lion Yard Development
Cambridge
Client: City of Cambridge
Architectural Review, Mar 1971, 147–8
Building Design **277**, 12 Dec 1975, 11
Baumeister **75**/2, Feb 1978, 150–3

1970–3
Music School, University of East Anglia
Norwich, Norfolk
Client: University of East Anglia
Architectural Review **157**/937, Mar 1975, 130–9

1970–5
IBM Head Office, phases 1 and 2
Cosham, Hampshire
Client: IBM UK Ltd
Arup Journal **13**/1, Mar 1978, 2–15
Building Design **473**, 23 Nov 1979, 28–30

1970–5
New buildings for Ampleforth
College
Ampleforth, North Yorkshire
Client: Ampleforth College

1970–6
Bush Lane House
Cannon Street, City of London
Client: Trafalgar House Ltd
Building **232**/6759 (9), 4 Mar 1977, 71–5
Arup Journal **12**/1, Nov 1977, 17–19
Structural Engineer **55**/2, Feb 1977, 75–85

1970–6
Sir Thomas White Building,
St John's College
Oxford
Client: St John's College, Oxford
Listed at grade II in 2017
Architectural Review **162**/970, Dec 1977, 350–63
Arup Journal **14**/1, Apr 1979, 2–14
Tyack, G 2005 Modern Architecture in an Oxford
College: St John's College, 1945–2005. Oxford:
OUP, 43–79

1971–5
Cambridge Central Library
Cambridge
Client: City of Cambridge

1971–6
Engineering and Metallurgy Building,
University of Oxford
Oxford
Client: University of Oxford
Tyack, G 1998 Oxford: An Architectural Guide.
Oxford: OUP, 319–20

1971–7
Greyfriars Bus Station★★
Northampton
Client: Northampton Borough
Council
Architecture East Midlands **63**, Mar/Apr 1976,
35–7

1971–9
Heavy Plate Shop, Support Buildings
and Training Centre, Portsmouth
Naval Dockyard
Portsmouth, Hampshire
Client: Portsmouth Naval Dockyard
Architects' Journal **163**/16, 21 Apr 1976, 793–806
Baumeister **75**/10, Oct 1978, 842–4

1972–5
Henry Wood Hall
Southwark, London
Client: Rehearsal Hall Ltd
Architects' Journal **161**/26, 25 Jun 1975, 1305–6

1972–5
Theatre Royal Glasgow, restoration
Glasgow
Client: Scottish Opera
Country Life **156**/4039, 28 Nov 1974, 1634–5
Architects' Journal **162**/43, 22 Oct 1975, 833–4
Arup Journal **11**/2, Jun 1976, 14–22

1972–6
Truman Headquarters
London
Client: Truman Ltd
Listed at grade II★ in 1994
Architects' Journal **164**/ 39, 29 Sep 1976, 575
Arup Journal **2**/12, Jun 1977, 2–13
Architectural Review **163**/974, Apr 1978, 222–8
Building **236**/7071 (3), 19 Jan 1979, 96–8

Truman's Brewery, 1972–6, rebuilt by Arup Associates as a foil for listed buildings on the site

1973–6
Gateway House 1
Basingstoke, Hampshire
Client: Wiggins Teape (UK) PLC
Listed at grade II in 2015
Architects' Journal **166**/34, 24 Aug 1977, 341–54
RIBA *Journal* **86**/8, Aug 1979, 363–5
Arup Journal **14**/3, Sep 1979, 2–13

1973–6
Lloyd's of London Administrative
Headquarters
Chatham, Kent
Client: Lloyd's of London
Listed at grade II in 2015
Architectural Review **159**/947, Jan 1976, 35
Architects' Journal **173**/5, 4 Feb 1981, 199–217
Blackmore, C 1990 *The Client's Tale*. London:
RIBA, 47–50

1973–8
CEGB South West Region
Headquarters
Bedminster, Bristol
Client: Central Electricity
Generating Board
Listed at grade II in 2015
Architectural Review **169**/26, Jul 1979, 9–22
Building **236**/7097 (29), 20 Jul 1979, 34–40
Architects' Journal **170**/7, 15 Aug 1979, 325–43
Aldous, T 2000 *C20: Bristol's Twentieth
Century Buildings.* Bristol: Redcliffe
Press, 83

1973–9
Cambridge Magistrates' Courts★★
Cambridge
Client: City of Cambridge
New Civil Engineer, 20 Apr 1978, 42

1974–7
IBM Computer Centre, phase 3
Cosham, Hampshire
Client: IBM UK Ltd

1976–8
Hinde House
Iver, Buckinghamshire
Client: Mr P Hinde

1976–8
Pears–Britten Music School
Snape, Suffolk
Client: Snape Maltings Foundation

1977–80
Trebor Factory★
Colchester, Essex
Client: Trebor Ltd
Architects' Journal **173**/2, 3 Jun 1981, 1049–66

1977–82
Babergh District Council Offices
Hadleigh, Suffolk
Client: Babergh District Council
Architectural Review **173**/1039, Sep 1983, 62–7

1978–82
IBM new Head Office
Cosham, Hampshire
Client: IBM UK Ltd
Building Design **473**, 23 Nov 1979, 28–30
Arup Journal **17**/3, Oct 1982, 13–19
Architectural Review **174**/1041, Nov 1983, 46–57

Babergh District Council Offices, Hadleigh,
council chamber

1978–9
Buxton Opera House, restoration
Buxton, Derbyshire
Client: Buxton Opera House Ltd
Arup Journal **14**/2, Jul 1979, 22–3

1978–9
**IBM Systems Assembly Plant:
extension**
Havant, Hampshire
Client: IBM UK Ltd

1978–80
Eton College Swimming Pool
Eton, Buckinghamshire
Client: Eton College

1978–83
Briarcliff House (Leslie & Godwin
Offices)
Farnborough, Hampshire
Client: ITC Pension Trust Ltd
Architects' Journal **180**/36, 5 Sep 1984, 63–82
Arup Journal **20**/2, Summer 1985, 2–8
Architects' Journal **183**/7, 12 Feb 1986, 53–6

1979–81
Assembly Building and Offices
Reading, Berkshire
Client: Digital Equipment Ltd
Architects' Journal **177**/18, 4 May 1983, 51–66

1979–81
Bedford School, reconstruction
Bedford
Client: Bedford Charity (The Harpur
Trust)
RIBA Journal **88**/3, Mar 1981, 46

1981–2
Gateway House 2
Basingstoke, Hampshire
Client: Wiggins Teape (UK) PLC
Arup Journal **19**/2, Jun 1984, 2–9
Baumeister **81**/10, Oct 1984, 32–9
Architects' Journal **180**/46, 14 Nov 1984, 55–66

1981–4
Diplomatic Quarter Sports Club
Riyadh, Saudi Arabia
Client: Bureau of Foreign Affairs,
Kingdom of Saudi Arabia
Arup Journal **25**/1, Spring 1990, 23–6

1981–4
No. 1 Finsbury Avenue★
City of London
Client: Rosehaugh Greycoat Estates PLC
Listed at grade II in 2015
Building **247**/7341 (18), 4 May 1984, 46–8
Building Design **698**, 13 Jul 1984, 18–19
Architectural Review **177**/1059, May 1985, 21–30
Baumeister **82**/10, Oct 1985, 43–9
Arup Journal **21**/2, Summer 1986, 2–7

1982
National Gallery, proposed
extension★★★
Competition entry
London
Client: National Gallery Trustees

1982–4
International Garden Festival Hall★★
Liverpool
Client: Merseyside Development
Corporation
Architects' Journal **175**/22, 2 Jun 1982, 28–33
Building **247**/7340 (17), 27 Apr 1984, 43–50
Architectural Review **175**/1048, Jun 1984, 29–31
Demolished in 2006.

1982–6
Forbes Mellon Library, Clare College
Cambridge
Client: Clare College, Cambridge
Architects' Journal **176**/42, 20 Oct 1982, 32–5
Building Design **791**, 13 Jun 1986, 12
Arup Journal **22**/3, Autumn 1987, 7–12

Briarcliff House

1985–7
**Stockley Park: master plan and
phase 1 development**
Hillingdon, London
Client: Stockley Park Consortium Ltd
Architects' Journal **179**/15, 11 Apr 1984, 37
Building **247**/7371 (48), 30 Nov 1984, 8
Building **250**/7448 (23), 6 Jun 1986, 42–4
Arup Journal **22**/1, Spring 1987, 22–3

1985–8
Nos. 2–3 Finsbury Avenue
City of London
Client: Rosehaugh Stanhope
Developments

1985–8
Broadgate Office Development★
City of London
Client: Rosehaugh Stanhope Devel-
opments
Hunting, P, Malt, D, Bennett, J and Gray, C
1991 Broadgate and Liverpool Street Station. London:
Rosehaugh Stanhope Developments
Architectural Review **181**/1083, May 1987, 47–51
Building **252**/7496 (20), 15 May 1987, 64–5
Building **252**/7497 (21), 22 May 1987, 80–1
Building **252**/7498 (22), 29 May 1987, 60–1
Architects' Journal **187**/1, 6 Jan 1988, 22–5
Building Design **875**, 4 Mar 1988, 14–16
Architects' Journal **190**/15, 11 Oct 1989, 79–81
Redevelopment is ongoing and
several of the blocks have now been
demolished (see Chapter 3).

1986–9
**Paternoster Square,
master plan**★★★
Competition entry
Client: Paternoster Properties
Arup Associates 1998 Paternoster: The Master
Plan. London: Arup Associates

Architects' Journal **187**/27, 6 Jul 1988, 24–5
Architects' Journal **187**/47, 23 Nov 1988, 9–10
Building **253**/7575 (48), 25 Nov 1988, 19–21
Architectural Review **183**/1091, Jan 1988, 19–20

1986–91
Legal & General House
Banstead, Surrey
Client: Legal & General
Listed at grade II in 2018
Arup Journal **27**/4, Winter 1992/3, 3–9
Franklin, G and Harwood, E 2017
Post-Modern Buildings in Britain. London:
Batsford, 92–3

1986–2000
**Imperial War Museum,
redevelopment**
London
Client: Imperial War Museum
Architects' Journal **190**/7, 16 Aug 1989, 22–4
Architects' Journal **199**/5, 2 Feb 1994, 14–15
Arup Journal **23**/4, Winter 1988/9, 2–6
Arup Journal **37**/2, 2002, 42–7
RIBA Journal **96**/9, Sep 1989, 80–5

1987–90
**Goodwood: master plan,
restaurant and Sussex Stand**
Goodwood, West Sussex
Client: Goodwood Racecourse Ltd
Architecture Today **11**, Sep 1990, 66–73
Arup Journal **27**/2, Summer 1992, 21–3

1987–91
Royal Life Offices
Peterborough, Cambridgeshire
Client: Royal Life Holdings Ltd
Arup Journal **26**/3, Autumn 1991, 3–10
Architectural Review **190**/1143, May 1992, 44–53

1988–9
Stockley Park Arena
Hillingdon, London
Client: Stockley Park Consortium Ltd
Architects' Journal **192**/5, 1 Aug 1990, 30–41

1988–90
123 Buckingham Palace Road Office
Development
London
Client: Greycoat London Estates Ltd
Building Design **188**, 3 Jun 1988, 24–5
Building Design **189**, 8 Jul 1988, 3

1989–90
Tennis Pavilion, Wentworth Golf Club
Virginia Water, Surrey
Arup Journal **27**/4, Winter 1992/3, 3

Clubhouse, Wentworth Golf Club***
Virginia Water, Surrey

1989–91
Copthorne Hotel
Newcastle upon Tyne
Client: Copthorne Hotels (Newcastle) Ltd
Architecture Today **23**, Nov 1991, 24–26, 29

1988–91
Lloyds Bank Offices
Bristol
Client: Lloyds Bank PLC
Building Design **1039**, 14 Jun 1991, 14–15
Architects' Journal **194**/16, 16 Oct 1991, 32–9, 42–5
Arup Journal **29**/3, 1994, 19–23

1993–9
Gro Laboratories and Offices
Newtown, Wales
Client: Development Board for Rural
Wales
Arup Journal **32**/3, 1997, 16–17

1993–2000
**City of Manchester Stadium
(now Etihad Stadium)**
Manchester
Building **267**/8231(16), 26 Apr 2002, 38–44
Architects' Journal **215**/19, 16 May 2002, 24–35
Arup Journal **36**/1, 2003, 25–36
Arup Journal **38**/2, 2003, 47–51

1995–8
The Square, Stockley Park
Client: Stockley Park Consortium Ltd
Architects' Journal **205**/11, 20 Mar 1997, 29–37
Arup Journal **33**/3, 1998, 3–8

1996–2006
Plantation Place
City of London
Client: British Land PLC
Architects' Journal **204**/5, 1 Aug 1996, 8–9
Building **269**/8340 (27), 9 Jul 2004, 54–6
Architecture Today **151**, Sep 2004, 58–77
Arup Journal **40**/2, 2005, 34–43

1997–9
Watling House
City of London
Client: British Land PLC
Arup Journal **36**/1, 2001, 36–8

1999–2007
Arup Campus
Solihull, West Midlands
Client: Ove Arup & Partners
Architects' Journal **215**/7, 21 Feb 2002, 24–35

2000
Battersea Power Station master plan***
London
Client: Parkview International PLC

Further reading

General works

Harwood, E 2015 *England's Post-War Listed Buildings*. London: Batsford

Harwood, E 2015 *Space, Hope and Brutalism*. New Haven, CT: Yale University Press

Harwood, E, Powers, A and Saumarez Smith, O (eds) 2013 *Oxford and Cambridge* (Twentieth Century Architecture 11). London: Twentieth Century Society

Hughes, N, Lewison, G and Wesley, T 1964 *Cambridge New Architecture*. Cambridge: self-published

Jones, P 2006 *Ove Arup: Masterbuilder of the Twentieth Century*. New Haven, CT and London: Yale University Press

Powers, A 2007 *Britain* (Modern Architectures in History). London: Reaktion Books

Saint, A 2007 *Architect and Engineer: A Study in Sibling Rivalry*. New Haven, CT and London: Yale University Press

Tonks, N (ed) 2012 *Ove Arup: Philosophy of Design, Essays 1942–1981*. Munich and London: Prestel

Tyack, G 1998 *Oxford: An Architectural Guide*. Oxford: OUP

General studies of Arup Associates

Brawne, M 1983 *Arup Associates: The Biography of an Architectural Practice*. London: Lund Humphries

Davies, C 1989 'Fast building: milestone or millstone?' (Interview with Peter Foggo). *Architects' Journal* **190**/15, 11 Oct 1989, 79–81

Dobney, S (ed) 1994 *Arup Associates: Selected and Current Works*. Mulgrave: Images Publishing Group

Goulet, P and Dowson P 1979 'Arup Associates'. *Architecture Intérieure Créé* **173**, Sep/Oct 1979, 80–7

MacCormac, R et al 1977 'Arup Associates'. *A&U* **12**/85, Dec 1977, 63–150

Powell, K 2013 *Arup Associates 50*. London: Arup Associates

Powell, K 2017 'Sir Philip Henry Manning Dowson' in Cannadine, D (ed) *Oxford Dictionary of National Biography*. Oxford: OUP. www.oxforddnb.com (Accessed Jan 2018)

Melvin, J, Lipton, S, MacCormac, R and Bennetts, R 1994 'A Modernist in Arcadia' (feature on the work of Peter Foggo). *Building Design*, 12 Aug 1994, 9–16

Writings by members of Arup Associates

Arup, O 1966 'Art and architecture: the architect–engineer relationship' (Gold Medal address). RIBA Journal **73**/8, 7 Aug 1966, 350–9

Arup, O 1980 'My architectural theory'. RIBA Journal **87**/11, Nov 1980, 43–4

Bennetts, R 2011 'Broadgate: an architect's perspective'. C20 Magazine, Autumn 2011, 8–9

Dowson, P 1966 'The architect's approach to architecture'. Arup Journal, May 1966, 9–19

Dowson, P 1968 'A room of one's own'. Architectural Design **38**/4, Apr 1968, 164–72

Dowson, P 1982 'Architecture in crisis'. Transactions of the RIBA **1**/1, 1982, 157–61

Dowson, P 2010 Fragments and Ambushes. Privately published

Foggo, P 1985 'Pilgrim's progress: reactions to Sir Charles Barry's Reform Club and some parallels with the work of Arup Associates'. Architects' Journal **181**/9, 27 Feb 1985, 30–2

Sturgis, T nd Memories of the 1960s at Arup Associates. Typescript sent to the author

Sugden, D 1968 'The anatomy of the factory'. Architectural Design, Nov 1968, 513–52

Sugden, D 1986 'The skeletal frame from Arkwright to Arup'. Baukultur **5**, 1986, 3–14

Obituaries

Anon 2014 Obituary of Philip Dowson. Daily Telegraph, 14 Sep 2014

Anon 2014 Obituary of Philip Dowson, The Times, 3 Oct 2014

Brown, D J 2006 Obituary of Ronald Hobbs, Independent, 7 Feb 2006

Dowson, P 1993 'Peter Foggo: anti-establishment prince among architects'. Architects' Journal **198**/2, 14 Jul 1993, 28–9

Glancey, J 2014 Obituary of Philip Dowson. The Guardian, 5 Sep 2014

Rowntree, D 2016 Obituary of Derek Sugden. The Guardian, 13 Jan 2016

Zunz, J 2006 Obituary of Ronald Hobbs. Arup Bulletin, Mar 2006

The Twentieth Century Society

Without the Twentieth Century Society an entire chapter of Britain's recent history was to have been lost. It was alert when others slept. It is still crucial!
SIMON JENKINS, WRITER, HISTORIAN, JOURNALIST

The Twentieth Century Society campaigns for the preservation of architecture and design in Britain from 1914 onwards and is a membership organisation which you are warmly invited to join and support.

The architecture of the twentieth century has shaped our world and must be part of our future; it includes bold, controversial, and often experimental buildings that range from the playful Deco of seaside villas to the Brutalist concrete of London's Hayward Gallery. The Twentieth Century Society produces many publications of its own to increase knowledge and understanding of this exciting range of work. The Twentieth Century Architects series has enabled the Society to extend its reach through partnership, initially with RIBA Publishing and now with Historic England, contributing the contacts and expertise needed to create enjoyable and accessible introductions to the work of architects who deserve more attention. In the process, the books contribute to the work of protecting buildings from demolition or disfigurement.

We propose buildings for listing, advise on restoration and help to find new uses for buildings threatened with demolition. Join the Twentieth Century Society and not only will you help to protect these modern treasures, you will also gain an unrivalled insight, through our magazine, journal and events programme, into the ground-breaking architecture and design that helped to shape the century.

For further details and to join online, see **www.c20society.org.uk**

CATHERINE CROFT
DIRECTOR

Other titles in the series

Ahrends, Burton and Koralek
Kenneth Powell
Apr 2012
978-1-85946-166-2

Aldington, Craig and Collinge
Alan Powers
Nov 2009 (*out of print*)
978-1-85946-302-4

Stephen Dykes Bower
Anthony Symondson
Dec 2011
978-1-85946-398-7

Chamberlin, Powell & Bon
Elain Harwood
Nov 2011
978-1-85694-397-0

Wells Coates
Elizabeth Darling
Jul 2012
978-1-85946-437-3

Frederick Gibberd
Christine Hui Lan Manley
978-1-84802-273-7

Howell Killick Partridge & Amis
Geraint Franklin
Jun 2017
978-1-84802-275-1

McMorran & Whitby
Edward Denison
Oct 2009
978-1-85946-320-8

John Madin
Alan Clawley
Mar 2011
978-1-85946-367-3

Robert Maguire & Keith Murray
Gerald Adler
Mar 2012
978-1-85946-165-5

Leonard Manasseh & Partners
Timothy Brittain-Catlin
Dec 2010
978-1-85946-368-0

Powell & Moya
Kenneth Powell
Apr 2009
978-1-85946-303-1

Ryder and Yates
Rutter Caroll
Apr 2009
978-1-85946-266-9

Alison and Peter Smithson
Mark Crinson
Jun 2018
978-1-84802-352-9

Forthcoming titles

Ernö Goldfinger
Elain Harwood and Alan Powers
978-1-84802-274-4

F X Verlade
Andrew Crompton and
Dominic Wilkinson
978-1-84802-548-6

Illustration credits

The author and publisher have made every effort to contact copyright holders and will be happy to correct, in subsequent editions, any errors or omissions that are brought to their attention.

© **Arup Associates**
pp xiii, 4 top, 7 (273/813002), 9 bottom (365/1714/004), 12, 16 (175), 17 (589/019), 18 (319/541/007 © Martin Charles), 19 (141014), 21 top (211/002), 21 bottom (211/004), 25 (334/252/005), 31 right (114/007), 39 (517), 42 (1573/01), 43 (624/002), 49 (110/005), 54 (133/001), 55 (345/126/001), 56 (618/011), 57 (618/002), 64 (435/008), 69 (636/016), 72 (219/06), 76 (50485/032), 77 (39022/001), 78 (816/015), 85 bottom (224/014), 94 (203/887-54/049), 96 (39038/314), 109 (39048/088), 112 (762/049), 113 (762/011), 115 (260/900/001), 117 (673/004), 120 (927/024), 123 (899/001/ invert), 125 top (56299/003), 125 bottom (56299/287), 128 (39014/011) and 129 (39087/035 © Peter Cook)

© **CIBA** pp 8 bottom (964/004) and 9 top (1501/001)

© **Dowson family** p 6

© **Alastair Fair** p 27

© **Historic England Archive (photographer Steve Baker)**
pp xix (DP184664), 46 (DP184666), 86–87 (DP188589), 88 (DP188626), 110 (DP184694), 122 top (DP184705), 122 bottom (DP184693), 140 (DP184681) and 149 (DP184675)

© **Historic England Archive (photographer Anna Bridson)**
pp 89 (DP197078), 90 (DP197082), 91 (DP197080), 118 (DP197086) and 119 (DP197088)

© **Historic England Archive (photographer James O Davies)**
Frontispiece (DP148497), pp vi (DP166043), xvi–xvii (DP167199), xxii (DP158111), 13 (DP180664), 15 top (DP158109), 15 bottom (DP195411), 20 (DP195666), 22–23 (DP195657), 26 (DP195312), 28–29 (DP195316), 31 left (DP195321), 33 (DP148493), 34–35 (DP195328), 38 (DP195329), 41 (DP137910), 44 (DP167197), 45 (DP099589), 47 (DP196510), 52 (DP162789), 58–59 (DP181999), 58 bottom (DP181989), 61 (DP162764), 62–63 (DP162762), 66–67 (DP166086), 68 (DP166034), 92–93 (AA047307), 98 (DP101710), 100–101 (DP136407), 102 (DP136400), 103 right (DP101712), 104 (DP101717), 126 (DP196132), 130–131 (DP196497), 144 (DP162866) and 147 (DP163178)

© **Historic England Archive (photographer Derek Kendall)**
pp 79 (DP132133) and 80 (DP130900)

© **Historic England Archive (photographer Patricia Payne)**
pp 50 (DP217313), 107 (DP187814, 108 (DP217162) and 148 (DP187819)

© **Historic England Archive (photographer Chris Redgrave)**
Front cover (DP183593),
pp xii (DP183602), 71 (DP183586),
73 (DP183591), 74 (DP183596),
82–83 (DP183572), 84 (DP183578),
85 top (DP183580), 95 (DP183600)
and 106 (DP182651)

© **Historic England Archive (photographer Peter Williams)**
p 2 MF99/0636/00005

© **RIBA collections** pp xiv (2647/14), 4 bottom (86945), 8 top (4813) and 60 (57449)

© **Sugden family** p 5, 103 and back cover

Index

Illustrations are indicated by page numbers in **bold**.